The Best
Women's Stage Monologues
of 2008

Edited and with a Foreword by
Lawrence Harbison

MONOLOGUE AUDITION SERIES

A SMITH AND KRAUS BOOK

Published by Smith and Kraus, Inc.
177 Lyme Road, Hanover, NH 03755
www.SmithandKraus.com

First Edition: February 2009
10 9 8 7 6 5 4 3 2 1
Cover illustration by Lisa Goldfinger
Cover and text design and production by Julia Hill Gignoux

The Monologue Audition Series
ISBN-13 978-1-57525-619-1 / ISBN-10 1-57525-619-3
Library of Congress Control Number: 2008941388

NOTE: These monologues are intended to be used for audition and class study; permission is not required to use the material for those purposes. However, if there is a paid performance of any of the monologues included in this book, please refer to the Rights and Permissions pages 104-106 to locate the source that can grant permission for public performance.

To receive prepublication information about upcoming Smith and Kraus books and information about special promotions, send us your e-mail address at info@smithandkraus.com with a subject line of MAILING LIST. You may receive our annual catalogue, free of charge, by sending your name and address to *Smith and Kraus Catalogue, PO Box 127, Lyme, NH 03768. Call toll-free (888) 282-2881 or visit us at SmithandKraus.com.*

CONTENTS

FOREWORD

In these pages, you will find a rich and varied selection of monologues from recent plays. Many are for younger performers (teens through thirties) but there are also some excellent pieces for women in their forties and fifties, and even a few for older performers. Many are comic (laughs), many are dramatic (generally, no laughs). Some are rather short, some are rather long. All represent the best in contemporary playwriting.

Several of these pieces are by playwrights whose work may be familiar to you such as Don Nigro, Nilo Cruz, Lee Blessing, Theresa Rebeck, Paul Rudnick, Adam Bock, José Rivera and Stephen Belber; others are by exciting up-and-comers like Jim Knabel, Peter Sinn Nachtrieb, Quira Alegría Hudes, Caitlyn Montanye Parrish, Jenny Schwartz, Qui Nguyen, Kate Fodor, Young Jean Lee and Brett C. Leonard. All are representative of the best of contemporary writing for the stage.

Most of the plays from which these monologues have been culled have been published and, hence, are readily available from the publisher/licensor or from theatrical book stores such as Drama Book Shop in New York. A few plays may not be published for a while, in which case contact the author or his agent for a copy of the entire text of the monologue that suits your fancy. Information on publishers/rights holders may be found in the Rights and Permissions section in the back of this anthology.

Break a leg in that audition! Knock 'em dead in class!

— *Lawrence Harbison*
Brooklyn, N.Y.

AND HER HAIR WENT WITH HER

Zina Camblin

Comic
Keisha, twenties, Black

Keisha is talking to her friend Jasmine about "Black Compulsive Disorder" and what she intends to do about it.

KEISHA: Black Obsessive Compulsive! You've seen it on *Seinfeld*, and *Frazier*, but us B.O.C.'s are in full effect. We're just closeted cause our people don't put up with that shit! "Keisha let me get a lick of your ice cream cone" . . . "What you mean no?" Can you get a spoon? "Mutha fucka! I just want one lick. Why you gotta be all stingy?" I'm not being stingy. I just don't want mouth bacteria on my cone. So then I hear: "Crazy-ass. Black folks ain't supposed to be actin' like that. You got that white-people mental disease. What's that shit called? Obsolete, obtuse complexion — some shit — that's what you got." *(Starts coughing.)* Ah man, I can't take this cough. It's a deep one. Must have caught it from homeboy on the bus. Why is it that people find this an acceptable thing to do? *(She sneezes without covering her mouth.)* Or this? *(She coughs without covering her mouth.)* Now I'm sick. Even though I held my breath for twenty seconds. That's the exact time it takes for germs to disintegrate after they've been released from their host body. People don't understand the danger of germs. Did ya see the movie "Outbreak"? Did you see all them nasty-ass monkeys? That's why I had to start my own company, B.O.C. Inc. This germ stuff is deeper than you think. My company is dedicated to the survival of our people. *(Jasmine laughs.)* I'm serious. Think about it. What is black peoples' primary mode of transportation in this city?

. . . That's right. Public transportation. Moving germ receptacles! What kind of restaurants line the streets of our black neighborhoods? Organic markets? No. McDonalds, Wendy's, Burger King.

Where are food servers the least likely to wash their hands? Fast food restaurants. It's a plan! They're killing us off. Why do you think health care ain't free? What community suffers the most? Blacks and Latinos. Doctors ain't gonna protect us!

(Takes out sanitizing wipes and begins to clean her hands.)

AND HER HAIR WENT WITH HER
Zina Camblin

Comic
Denise, twenties, Black

*Denise talks to her friend Jasmine about her trials and tribulations
at her various jobs.*

DENISE: It's fine for a nine to five. Mr. Kaufman is a real slave master. He
calls me his secretary, but I'm really a personal assistant. *(Cell phone
rings again.)* Kaufman Realtors. No he's not in yet. Maybe he did,
but I'm sitting in front of his office door, and he's not here. Hold
on. I'll transfer you. *(Hangs up phone.)* I can't believe he gives his
clients my cell phone number. This is my fifth job this month. I've
been fired four times in one month, and none of the reasons have
been in my control.

    . . . I'll get there when I get there. Massa doesn't get there until
eleven anyway. At first I was working at a marketing company. You
know, telephone stuff. The guy in the cubicle next to mine, we'll
just call him Jeff cause that's his real name, he used to throw these
paper airplanes into my cubicle with vulgar messages on them. I
wanna stick my plane in your terminal, let me slide down your run-
way, you know freaky stuff. When I finally reported it I was told
that the tweed knee length skirts I wear to work were too revealing
and it was my own fault. Can you believe it — and Jeff turned out
to be the bosses nephew — so nothing happened to him. Looking
up my skirt, talking dirty to me at my job? So then I had to go
down a peg and work at Shoe World. Not that there's anything
wrong with shoes. But people got some nasty feet.

    This older guy comes in to try on some athletic sandals and
insists that I be the one to put them on his feet. That wouldn't have
been a problem if he hadn't of had fungus growing out of his toes

and rotting toe nails which were causing me to dry heave. I refused to help him into his sandals and was fired on the spot. *(Cell phone rings.)* Kaufman Realtors. We're closed for the day. I know it's only 9:30. We had a bomb threat. *(She hangs up.)* So then I had to go even lower down on the ladder and work at a coffee shop. We'll call it Starchucks to protect its identity. Things started off well. By the third day I could make any drink off the menu with no mistakes and run the register. My boss said I had a lot of potential and he could see me being promoted to manager within six months. Everything was good until this bitch on her cell phone comes in, orders I guess a decaf vanilla latte, and a bunch of pastries. Well after I get all the damn pastries I forgot if she said decaf or regular. When I asked her to repeat it, this lunatic took her cell phone from her ear and snapped at me, "I already told you once. Figure it out." So I made it a regular. Well she took two sips of it and started having convulsions. I was fired on the spot. *(Cell phone rings.)* Kaufman Realtors. I'm not his keeper. I don't know where the hell he is. *(She hangs up.)* Well a friend of mine worked at this bank and she said they needed tellers. This was a huge step for me so I applied and got the job. Now I don't have a car. I ride the bus to work. So my first day the bus breaks down. I'm late for work. I tell my boss it won't happen again. Second day a car runs a red light and side swipes the bus. I'm late again. My boss says he'll give me one more chance. Third day the bus is hijacked by a homeless man with an ax. I'm fired on the spot. My boss thinks I'm making it all up. He doesn't understand my luck with jobs. So that leads me to this job where Mr. Kaufman is accusing me of not taking the job seriously. Ain't that a bitch.

...AND WE ALL WORE LEATHER PANTS
Robert Attenweiler

Dramatic
Mary, twenties

Mary is speaking to her husband Jagger and has just revealed that she's lost/misplaced their baby, Ruble. She has a history of misplacing her children and Jagger asks "What happens?"

MARY: Oh, all the ones been in me once upon a time. Never lost track of a baby before Jagger. But did lose count. Lost count a' how many when I got up in double-digit kids. Not so unusual a girl my age fillin' a house, but I couldn't stop with the kids. Filled *that* house and *that* house and *that* one. Got to the point I couldn't sit down on the couch without hearin' a little cry and findin' one of my babies stuck under me — I'd pour out a Raisin Bran and two or three would tumble out of the box. So many, they'd hang from the pole in my closet and I don't have no choice but to drape my blouse over their soft little heads so as not to wrinkle 'em on the floor. But they lost patience with me. They began to use all fours and swear I seen 'em scurry up a wall to hide in shadow — conspirin' to drive me out. And one day they did — content they'd do a better job raisin' themselves than I could. I went back tonight. Several more got teeth now. Asked back in. Told 'em things would be different. That losin' Jagger n' my babies made me appreciate them. That I'd go back, name 'em all and these'd be names I'd remember. They just hissed. Jagger used to believe anything I'd tell him. But my beautiful little beasts wouldn't even give me that little moment when my wrong word makes me a beautiful world.

BEAUTY OF THE FATHER
Nilo Cruz

Dramatic
Marina, twenties

Marina is talking to her father about the day her mother died.

MARINA: Ah, Mamá had a hat like this one. It's lovely, isn't it?
. . . She looked so beautiful the day she died. No one would
think . . . She died with such grace. That afternoon she said, "Pass
me my purse. Let me look at my face in the mirror." She opened
her compact, looked at herself and said, "Oh, I look fine." Then she
asked me to play music. She said she only wanted to hear Fades.
And I played her Amalia Rodrigues. All of a sudden her face became
vibrant, as if she had reached into her purse and pulled out her last
strand of life. She got up and asked me to dance with her. "Listen
to that voice," she'd repeat over and over again. "Listen to the clarity of that voice." Then she sat in her chair and she took her last
breath listening to Amalia's voice.

And I was actually proud of myself that day. I didn't get hys-
terical or anything. I didn't call the doctor or the rescue right away.
Instead I took my time before she was taken away from me. I let the
music play on. I combed her hair and powdered her face.

I colored her lips and perfumed her neck. And I sat there and
looked at her as if she were a painting, because I tell you, Papá, she
looked like a masterpiece of life that was. And when the rescue
came, they wanted to know at what time this, at what time that.
And I wasn't much help. I told them she had just come back from
a dance — that my mother had just come back from Spain after
dancing with my father. *(Laughs.)* They must've thought I was mad.

THE BEEBO BRINKER CHRONICLES

Kate Moira Ryan and Linda S. Chapman

Dramatic
Beebo, twenties

> *Beebo has tried to pick up a woman she fancies but has been turned down. Here she tries again.*

BEEBO: BEEBO: Tell me baby. Tell me all about it.

   . . . Try baby. Try.

   . . . You don't need to tell me about it, because I already know. I've lived through it too. You fall in love. You're young, you're inexperienced. You fall, up to your ears and there's nobody to talk to, nobody to lean on. You're all alone with that great big miserable feeling and she's driving you out of your mind. Finally you give in to it and she's straight. End of story. End of soap opera. And then again, beginning of soap opera. That's all the village is honey, just one crazy little soap opera after another. All tangled up with each other, one piled on top of the next, ad infinitum Mary loves Jean, Jane loves Joan, Joan loves Jean and Beebo loves Laura. Doesn't mean a thing. It goes on forever. Where one stops another begins. I know most of the girls in here. I've probably slept with half of them, I've lived with half of the half I've slept with. What does it all come to? You know something baby? It doesn't matter. Nothing matters. You don't like me and that doesn't matter. Someday maybe you'll love me, and that won't matter either. Because it won't last. Not down here. Not anywhere in the world, if you're gay you'll never find peace, you'll never find Love. With a capital L. L for Love. L for Laura. L for Lust and L for the L of it L for Lesbian. L for let's, let's. Let's. How about it? Want to go home with Beebo?

THE BEEBO BRINKER CHRONICLES

Kate Moira Ryan and Linda S. Chapman

Dramatic
Marcie, twenties

> *Marcie has blown Laura off, but she offers an apology and a plea for her to come back to her.*

MARCIE: Laura, I'm going to tell you something. And you're going to listen.

    . . . I did an awful thing, Laura. And now it's eating me up. I've known for a while about you.

    . . . I couldn't help knowing. You couldn't hide it Laura. You couldn't come near me without showing how you felt. Those crazy moods. I've been around enough to know. I even told Burr what I suspected. I even bet Burr I could make a pass at you.

    . . . Laura I don't know why I did what I did. Lead you on. I guess I thought it would be a lot of kicks. And just now you told me how you felt and how you wanted me — Laura, I had no idea you could love like that. You made it beautiful. Laura, I'm ashamed. I played you for a fool and all the while you were an angel. Laura, I'd do anything for you. If I could love you the way you want me to, I'd do that. I'll even try if you want me to. Laura do whatever you want with me. I've hurt you so terribly. Hurt me back if it'll help. Do something. Do anything. Only don't cry. Only don't leave. Laura! Please come back!

BOATS ON A RIVER
Julie Marie Myatt

Dramatic
Sister Margaret, early sixties

> *Sister Margaret runs a shelter in Phnom Penh, Cambodia. Here she is berating Sidney, who has come to the country for the sex trade.*

SISTER MARGARET: This is my personal life. You're right. And there have been nights I've wished for nothing more than someone to go home to. Someone who I loved and could devote myself to; who I could talk to about myself. A warm body to hold . . . to be held. *(Clears her throat at this revealing confession . . .)* But that's not the choice I made with my life. I went in another direction. I don't regret it. I live with my choices quite comfortably . . . But I'm sorry . . . I cannot stand by and watch you destroy what I happen to believe — what I know — is very important. Your refuge. Your adult refuge. From here. You need your own refuge, Sidney . . . Love and kindness . . . we both made choices, Sidney. But this is your personal life too and you're killing it. You marry a sex worker, have two kids with her, and leave her . . . and you want to tell me that your work and personal life are not a bit at odds at the moment? And I thought you were a smart man. Please . . . Get off your high horse, Sidney. Stop acting like the only thing people want from you, and the only thing you have to offer people, is fixing them. What makes you so special? You have a magic potion, you have a wand, or some kind of super powers that I haven't seen? . . . No one has asked you to fix them, Sidney. Not your wife, or these girls . . . That's not what we're here for . . . We're here to give them food and shelter and aid and love and a future . . . That's all we can do . . . You think you can mend all the loss and all the scars, and you will fail . . . I promise. You will fail. You can't do it. All the factories in this country couldn't sew these little girls back together, make it look like nothing has changed, nothing is broken . . . There are too many scars and there's not enough thread or stitches to go around. We can't mend anyone back to someone they might have been, we can only hold them together as they are . . . wounds and all . . . And that's alright . . . That's wonderful, actually. Your wife had a a horrible childhood, and it had nothing to do with you. She got hurt and you weren't there. Get over yourself and get her some help . . . Send Max . . . Send me . . . But please go home and be her friend, and stop trying to make her all better.

A BODY OF WATER
Lee Blessing

Dramatic
Wren, twenties

Wren tells Moss she knows he killed his eleven-year-old daughter.

WREN: *(Rising, staring out the window.)* One bright, sunny, frozen day, you made a 911 call to your local authorities. Robin was missing from her home — your home. Not that far from here. This is your summer place, by the way. You claimed initially that she hadn't come home the night before. You thought she was at a sleep-over, but when she didn't come home that morning, you called, and . . . well, she was just gone. Police came, took a few pictures, poked all around. Because you're a judge, they bent the rules and put out an immediate missing person's, Amber Alert — the whole package. After all, you seemed so *sure* she was missing and not just with friends, or a boy or whatever. You were right. When the ice came off the lake three months later, there she was: a few shreds of clothes, a bracelet, ankle chain — though not much ankle.

. . . But there's no disguising a crushed skull. So *bap*! Murder investigation. And the funny thing was, there were no suspects. Except you.

. . . Funny thing about the sleep-over. It didn't happen. Her little friend got sick. So Robin did in fact flutter home that night at about — oh, eleven P.M. Dropped off by her friend's mom. She watched her go in. So you had to change your story. OK, you said, "We must have been asleep when she came home. We got confused." Awkward.

. . . Police had you in. You went voluntarily. Prominent jurist, woman of accomplishment — it was all very delicate, believe me. You told what you knew, the second version: She must have sneaked out.

. . . Problem was, where would she go? Exclusive neighborhood, cold night. Hell of a long walk anywhere. She was eleven.

Didn't take a very heavy coat. She didn't know anyone with a car. Except you. Speaking of cars, your neighbor — the insomniac? — claims to have heard one leave your place that night at, golly — two A.M. So that interested police, given there were no signs of forced entry and you denied going anywhere. When they wanted to search your home again, you made them get a warrant. Didn't find anything. Practically painted the joint with Luminol — no blood. Naturally you posted a reward, flyers, created the "Have you seen Robin?" website. Didn't really help, though. Everyone in the world thinks you did it. *(A long beat.)*

. . . Lots of theories, of course. Why no blood? My personal favorite is that one or both of you smothered her. Then you got all panicky, the way people do, and you made a plan. One or both of you gathered up your poor, little dead girl, wrapped her in heavy-duty plastic, since it *was* a heavy duty, tossed her in the trunk and drove her up here to this lake. Then — and this was smart, I'll give you this — then and only then did you bash her head in. Did a good job of it. Left forensics with a classic conundrum. Where's the blood? Not in your house. Anyhow, you slipped her in the lake, one or both of you, drove home and called the cops the next morning. Oh, lucky for you — big cold front came through that night. Froze that lake up as solid as . . . well, ice. By the time Robin came up a-bob-bob-bobbin', there wasn't much left of Robin.

BOOM
Peter Sinn Nachtrieb

Dramatic
Barbara, thirties to forties

Barbara is a lecturer of sorts, here to tell us how the world ended centuries ago. Here, she talks about how she came to be.

BARBARA: Ohhhhh. Oh oh oh. There is trouble!

   The food is gone, the air is thin, the fan has really been hit! What oh what are they going to do? And it's gotta be something
   [Huge!!]
   I would really like to tell you how I was conceived.
(She looks to see if the coast is clear.)
   It was a hot sticky sticky hot day. The type of day where you are hoping for someone to breathe on your face for a bit of wind. The type of day when your outstretched hand disappears in a haze of vapor. The type of day when clothing becomes more of a nuisance than a much-appreciated social construct.
   My mother-to-be was by the shore, sprawled under a tree whose shade offered nothing. The water looked refreshing but the violent surf, fear of the unseen, and a mild allergy to salt kept her from moving too close. She lay back on the hot sand, opening her body wide so that any movement of air would have maximum contact.
   My father-to-be was in the sea, a short ways away, theoretically hunting for food but really floating on his back and daydreaming. Oddly comfortable with his body image, he had stripped himself of all his clothes, save for a wristwatch he wore for sentimental reasons. His dreams were vivid. Having recently pledged to not actively pleasure himself in an effort to bring more focus and productivity to his life, his dreams skewed towards filling the void that his hands had left.
   He dreamt his naked body was swimming in a pool filled with cool, vibrating, lubricated marbles that gently rolled and rubbed and activated his exterior, asking it to be alert. Reaching out

13

through the moistness he touched skin reaching out towards his. Not his own, like a leg he forgot about. It was the skin of my mother.

Not her *actual* skin, or course, which was . . .

[on the shore]

It was what he had envisioned for years to coat her flesh. Warm and wet, colorful and perfect. The imaginary touching grew, back and forth motions intensified, a feeling so beautiful and over-whelming surged until my father-to-be, in his dream, and in the water, exploded.

My mother-to-be heard a slight popping noise above the surf, glanced outwards but could only see a discoloration of the haze, and she felt particles land on her skin that felt refreshingly cool.

What she did not see was the fertile fluid that had erupted out of my father-to-be one hundredth of a second before he himself erupted pushed by the energy of the blast quickly and invisibly towards the shore where the smallest of portions had just the right angle to land inside my mother-to-be, swim with passion and feist into her core, fertilize an egg, and make me.

It took a number of years to figure out how that all happened, and it's been a party story ever since. I've embellished it of course, as we are wont to do, but I remain faithful to the story's intent. I am passionate about my stories!

(She looks up.)

PASSIONATE!

I'm sorry. I'm really *really* not supposed to be . . .

[talking]

I just thought . . . I could share how this is

[personal . . .]

The theme, the resilience of life, against all odds blah blah blah and such . . .

(Barbara stifles a tear.)

I'm sorry.

It's just . . . this is the last day I get to do this.

BOOM
Peter Sinn Nachtrieb

Dramatic
Jo, twenties

> *Jo has answered a personal ad placed by a marine biologist. She meets him at his lab and he tells her that the world is about to end and she and he will be the only ones to survive Armageddon.*

JO: I wish I'd been a cheerleader instead of smart and different! I'd have a boyfriend. And we'd have gone on a nice date tonight. We would have had hot heterosexual sex.

I wish I knew how to meet normal people, have normal experiences and just, maybe, have a moment where something mildly pleasurable happens . . . but instead, I meet a faggy psycho like you into some Road Warrior meets Survivor fantasy apocalypse whateverthefuckthisis bullshit where you want to pretend you're lucky when nobody else is.

You're not a lucky person! And neither am I.

We're the kind of people who get the data wrong, who get stuck in the basement lab, whose bodies sabotage their intentions and make them hostile and horny at the same time. So go fuck yourself and your fish and your fantasy and see —

— Ya later!

BOOM
Peter Sinn Nachtrieb

Dramatic
Barbara, thirties to forties

Barbara is a lecturer of sorts, here to tell us how the world ended centuries ago. Here, she describes the exact moment of Armageddon.

BARBARA: I wanted you to know that the actual noise was louder. And there was a lot of shaking of things. Some flames. Dust. Miscellany falling from elevated places. Chaos. Terror.
(A gesture of chaos and terror, maybe toppling a few things.)
    We have tried our best to reproduce that here. Alas, there's only so much we can do. What with the limitations: Physical, cognitive, budgetary. I just wanted to underscore the . . . girth of the moment. Big Girth.
(A gesture of large girth.)
    This is, in fact, that well known moment in time. What we now refer to as "The Boom"? Everyone is familiar with that term? I will assume your silence or words mean "yes."
    We're all familiar with the general circumstances of the event? That he was correct? The fish were correct? The impact did indeed [occur?]
    And most everything, almost all forms of life, you know, just . . .
    [ceased to live]
    Pretty unfortunate, really. That there are moments in time when everything has to go like that. Dolphins especially. But, alas, it is a brutal history that we are all a part of.
(With increasing passion.)
    A history that goes back millions and millions and millions of years. Back to that fresh rock, angry water, that sludgy mix of young amino acids sloshing about in the soup with reckless handsome

abandon until CRACK! The perfect bolt of energy in the perfect spot and there you have it: The world's first protein!

Motherfucker!

So begins this amazing story of change, of innovation, of great catastrophe, of LIFE. MY GOD WHAT A STORY OF LIFE IT IS!

I'm Barbara.

(A gesture towards her tag.)

Just in case you

[forget.]

I'm sitting over there. I'm . . . I'm really not supposed to be talking at all.

(She laughs.)

But sometimes what we're supposed to do

[isn't what we should do]

Right? Right? Right.

"The Boom." It's not just about a loud noise. It's the event: a sudden, radical change in the state of things.

THE BUTCHER OF BARABOO

Marisa Wegrzyn

Comic
Gail, forties

> *Gail, a policewoman, is having difficulty recording her suicide tape.*

> *Late that night. Gail at the kitchen table with a tape recorder and gun.*

GAIL: *(Hits 'record' button.)* Okay. Hey. If my handwriting weren't all chicken scratch I'd leave a note but, uh. Crud. That's stupid.
(Stop, rewind, record.)

Hi. This is Gail. Um. If you're listening to this, it means, um. y'know, I'm probably dead. On the floor. Or something. No.
(Stop, rewind. record.)

Hi. Um. Blehhh. Poop.
(Stop, rewind, record.)

Let's see, uh. Hi. Gail here. These are my last words. Um, first to Eddie. You're a bastard for sleeping around with cocktail waitresses that Shirley or Susie or Sally. I let you follow your dreams and you didn't give two halfshits about my dreams and I had dreams, whole dreams, not just halfshits of dreams, and you better believe I would not have encouraged your baseball dream had I known the steroids would squash your little sperms. To Valerie. You were never good enough for my brother and if you didn't kill him then you drove him to it and that's all I have to say about that. Though you do bring me good cuts of meat and you don't make me pay for them. So, thanks. Midge, you irritate me. A lot. But I know how much you like Billy Joel so you can have my records Glass Houses and 52nd Street. You're welcome to Piano Man, but it has a big scratch. And, also, have my collection of souvenir ashtrays, I've collected one from every state except Montana and Hawaii. And Delaware but *(Scoffs.)*. Sevenly, if you want my Peter Paul & Mary record your kids might like that, it's very wholesome. Donal: I don't have anything for you. You made fun of me when we were younger and you made me feel stupid and you set my teddy bear on fire. It's you who should've died instead of Frank. And if the lot of you think I haven't been very nice, then that's just the way I am and what I felt is what I felt and I can't change things now. The Crystal Meth I did gave me clarity and perspective, mostly on the ineffectiveness and wrong-headedness of our school district's anti-drug programs. *(Pause.)* I loved Frank and I miss him. I miss him so much. The other day, I drove to the lake, late, and the lake, it was frozen, and out there, I thought I saw Frank give me a wave before going under. It was my imagination I suppose. I'll have to live and die with that I suppose. And . . . Despite all the stuff I've said, I love most of you somehow, for some reason. That's it. Goodbye.

(Stop. Pause. Rewind. Play.)

CHRISTMAS BELLES

Jessie Jones, Nicholas Hope and Jamie Wooten

Comic
Geneva, sixties

> *Geneva is the jolly proprietor of a flower shop in a small Southern town.*

> *Christmas music plays over a crackling PA system. Lights come up on Miss Geneva Musgrave, sixties, the crusty proprietor of BooKoo BoKay, the only flower shop in Fayro, Texas, population 3,003. The shop is also the town bus depot. The phone rings. She answers.*

GENEVA: This is BooKoo BoKay. Whether you're sayin' "Get well soon," "I do" or "I'll never touch that woman again," say it with flowers. How can I help you? . . . Why, Tenny, how you doin'? . . . Actually, I'm waiting for the three twenty-five from Houston to bring my floral shipment. Nelda's funeral today cleaned me out. And speaking of which, if Nelda Lightfoot was half the psychic she claimed to be, how come she didn't know that runaway Christmas float was bearing down on her? . . . Yeah, up 'til then it was a real good parade. The float from Clovis Sanford's House of Meat was definitely my favorite, even though it turned out to be a killer . . . Oh, business is great. After all these years, I have found the key to success in the floral business: helium. Do you know I've tripled my Christmas orders by introducing the "Happy Birthday Jesus Balloon Bouquet"? Well, I sure have. And even my Greyhound franchise is startin' to pay off. Oh, hold on, Tenny. I got a bus just in from Brownsville . . . *(Into a microphone.)* Attención, Ladies and Gentlemen, Señores y Señoritas. Welcome and bienvenito to Fayro, Texas. We hope you'll do your holiday shopping para la entire familia while you're here. So let BoKoo BoKay help with any floral necessitas you may have. Merry Christmas and Feliz Navidad to y'all and yours! *(Back to the phone.)* I'm telling you, Tenny, all this success has helped take the sting out of not being asked to direct the church Christmas Program — for the first time in twenty-seven years . . . Evidently the Deacons thought the show needed new blood. I only hope Honey Raye Futrelle knows the mess she's getting into . . . You're right. I have to let it go. After all, it *is* Christmas. And to quote Tiny Tim, "God help us every one" . . . Of course I know it's really "God *bless* us every one," but girl, this is Fayro, Texas. And we need all the help we can get . . . *(Blackout.)*

CHRONICLES SIMPKINS WILL CUT YOUR ASS OFF
Rolin Jones

Dramatic
Jessica, thirties to forties

*Jessica is telling off a teacher at Chronicles' school for reporting her
for being in possession of drugs, for which she has been expelled.*

JESSICA: She'll be expelled. Principal Cody will ship her to another school
and she'll rule the tetherball court there and the same jealousies will
conspire to break her spirit. Pretty soon she'll be selling her body for
crack. Is that what you want? You want Chronicles smoking crack?
You want to ruin her life? Did you run out here to this small little
bit of asphalt, blowing your whistle, making wild accusations
because you're trying to justify your existence, Mr. Finkel? Because
you have failed to prepare your students, students like Billy Conn
for the coming world? A world that is surprising, and scary and yes,
occasionally unfair? It's something he can't find in the books you
make us read. And the lessons you draw up on the chalkboard. You
have to let children fall, Mr. Finkel. You have to let them fall and
get back up on their own. Chronicles is an outcast here, Mr. Finkel.
In exile everywhere she carries her Fun Dip. But from ten-thirty-
five to eleven o'clock and twelve thirty to one fifteen she feels safe.
When Chronicles steps into this circle, when she's hitting her high
arcing serves, and flying that ball over the heads of children more
privileged than her, for a brief moment in space and time, Mr.
Finkel, Chronicles Simpkins is immortal. And just witnessing it is a
thing of beauty. And you want to take that away from her. From us.
Shame on you, Mr. Finkel. Billy Conn was weak. That's what happened here.

THE CONSCIENTIOUS OBJECTOR
Michael Murphy

Dramatic
Coretta, thirties

> *Coretta Scott King speaks to a group in New York City shortly after*
> *her husband's assassination and shares with them some notes found*
> *in Dr. King's pocket pertaining to his stance on the war in*
> *Vietnam.*

CORETTA: My husband had been scheduled to speak here tonight. It was
on his calendar for quite some time. He said he could not turn down
an invitation to come back to New York to speak about this awful
war. I felt someone needed to keep the commitment. I can tell you
. . . People seemed . . . I think they were a little intimidated speakin'
in his place, I think, bein' so soon after . . . So they finally had to, well,
they asked if I'd do it. And, so . . . I can't say that my husband knew
exactly what he was gonna say to you tonight. But I want to tell you
he'd been thinkin' about it. I know because . . . I found this . . .
(Coretta unfolds a sheet of paper.)
In the pocket of his suit. The suit that he, that he wore to
Memphis. He must'a found a quiet moment or two in all the chaos
there to make some notes. But it was just that, a moment. Because
he folded this up and put it in his pocket to work on later. It's not
a speech. Just some thoughts. Knowing him, he'd have revised it a
dozen times and it would'a gotten maybe a little too long. Still . . .
I'd like to read it to you . . . He gave it a title: The Ten
Commandments of Vietnam.
(NOTE: This is taken from notes King made in Memphis which were
reported to have been found in the pocket of his jacket.)
They go like this . . . Thou shalt not believe the people we
claim to be fightin' for love us. Thou shalt not believe they are

grateful for our support. Thou shalt not believe they consider the insurgents who kill our soldiers to be 'terrorists'. Thou shalt not believe they support the government we've given them. Thou shalt not believe our government's figures on casualties and deaths. Thou shalt not believe our generals know best. Thou shalt not believe even our most sympathetic allies think what we are doin' is right. Thou shalt not believe that our enemy's victory means our defeat. Thou shalt not believe there are military solutions to political problems. Thou shalt not kill.

CUSTODY OF THE EYES
Anthony Giardina

Dramatic
Sheila, forties

Sheila has a son who has a rare disease which requires constant care. Here she tells a defrocked priest why she has resisted putting her son in an institution.

SHEILA: Father, I've noticed you won't look directly at me. Why is that? Priestly secret. I won't pry. *(Beat.)* I have a son, Father. He's eleven years old. He's never received communion. When I married, I had no particular religion, lapsed something, like the rest of the world, Catholic in my case. My husband thought he might be the one more likely to return to the fold in time, so we tilted toward Judaism when our son was born. My husband left us. He lives in Boston now. He's a social worker. Remarried. The only shred of Judaism left in our house is my son's lack of a foreskin. *(She smiles, acknowledges her very small joke.)* He's in a wheelchair, Father. *(She takes a cookie. It breaks in her hand as she tries to eat it. She has to catch it as she goes on.)* He was born with a disease you've never heard of. At the time, only six children in the world were thought to have it. He was not expected to make it to the age of three. He can't see. He is fed through a tube in his stomach because of a problem with reflux that can always threaten to suffocate him. There was a moment when Riley was three, when it became clear he might well survive for a number of years. It was suggested to me that he be institutionalized. "Placed" is actually the word they use. That it was the only way for me to have a life. To save my marriage, which at that point was understandably coming apart at the seams. There are good people, they said. You will stay connected. *(Beat.)* There I was, with a three year old boy and images of myself pushing him in a wheelchair for the rest of his life. My husband had left social work to come to this island and become a painter. Me, I'm a nurse. We had certain dreams, Father. It would have been the logical thing to let him go. *(Beat.)* You'll think this is odd. A "voice" appeared in my head. "Keep him," it said. Utterly clear. "Keep him." And then it disappeared. *(Beat.)* I have fought the good fight for eight years. My marriage ended. I've done it alone. And now I've reached a difficult patch. I won't go into why, it can't concern you. But one of the things it occurs to me I could do is try and involve Riley more in my life. I go to church now, I've come back. *(Checking with him.)* I am waiting for that voice to appear again, I suppose, that moment of unambiguous clarity. So, perhaps — I thought — he could come with me. And when I walk down the aisle to receive communion *(Again checking with him.)*, well, maybe he could come with me. It could be I'm fooling myself, but there's my thinking.

CUSTODY OF THE EYES
Anthony Giardina

Dramatic
Sheila, forties

> *Sheila has a son who has a rare disease which requires constant care. Here she tells a defrocked priest how this burden on her just may be God's test of her faith.*

SHEILA: When I chose to keep him at home, Father —
(She pauses, something difficult in this.)
    When I heard that voice eight years ago, it didn't come as a sporting challenge. It didn't come as a wager I could lose. I allowed it to change me, Father. You don't spend eleven years living day in, day out with a child and then act as though you can say, OK, enough, this is getting too damn hard. I am connected to him. I couldn't let him go now. *(Beat.)* Could you do that? Live without your relationship to your God? No? But what if God's crafty, Father? What if he wants to test us? Take us to the limit. Jesus in the desert, fasting. Wasn't that the moment when the devil came in? What if this is — excuse me — the devil talking to me? He's sitting beside me in the car, saying: What do you need this for? Go ahead. *(Beat.)* Because maybe — well, maybe this is one of God's odd ways — maybe we are near the end. Sometimes I get a strange inkling of that. Maybe there is only a little bit longer to go. And it stands to reason — to me — that that would be the moment when the pressure might build, and explode. Ever see Caravaggio's painting of Abraham sacrificing Isaac? So there's your old world patriarch Abraham. And in every classic Bible image he's got the long beard, the soulful eyes lifted to heaven: why, God, why do you ask me to do this? But in Caravaggio, who maybe knew a thing or two about how things work down here on earth, there's Abraham holding the knife with a look on his face like he can't *wait* to do the deed. And

poor Isaac is screaming, and even the lamb in the corner is looking terrified, and the angel sent by God is wearing a look that says: uh oh. Uh oh. Maybe God misjudges sometimes, Father. Being not quite human. He misjudges that desire we have to just be rid of it all. That impulse to say: *enough.* God must always be surprised. Uh oh. Too big a burden on that one . . . An angel came, yes. *(Beat.)* At the last moment. Am I correct? Stayed Abraham's hand. At the last moment. An angel. How God works. He sends angels.
(Beat.)
    Helpmates. Friends.

THE DRUNKEN CITY
Adam Bock

Dramatic
Jessica, twenties

Jessica tells us that she has called off her engagement.

JESSICA: *(To audience.)* I had everything. I had a ring. It was such a beautiful night the night Jason gave it to me. My hair was up like. And Jason looked so shiny and redfaced and he was smiling like at me like I was the only person anywhere anywhere anywhere. It was gonna be awesome. And. And we were going to buy a house. I'd already picked it out. It had a gazebo in the backyard. With screens. Where you could put a table in the summer.

　　Then slowly like a murmur that I didn't notice at first I couldn't hear it properly I kept hearing these two names. These two names over and over in different low voices. Jason and Jessica. Jessica and Jason.

　　What kind of name is Jessica anyways Who'd name their kid that? Jessica It's a stupid name.

　　It was humiliating. I gave my ring back to Jason. And suddenly all over again I had nothing all over again.
(Blinks.)

THE DRUNKEN CITY
Adam Bock

Dramatic
Marnie, twenties

> *Marnie tells us how she felt about telling her Dad that she has called off her engagement.*

MARNIE: My Dad

My Dad and I were upstairs wrapping birthday presents for my nephew and my niece,

they're twins, they're so cute, they both have noses that
(Pushes her nose.)

Cute. Cute. They are cute.

So we were upstairs and we were wrapping their presents and my Dad says "How're you doing?" and I burst into tears. I was just. And.

And I tried to explain it to him I said "Dad Gary ties his ties too tight." and he said "Uh huh?" and I said "Really really tight" and he looked at me He's such a nice guy my Dad Do you like your Dad? Me too. I love my Dad. My Dad looked at me and I wanted to say "I think I might have made a mistake I might have" but I was scared because he likes Gary and they both have Toyota Corollas and they both like watching TV together and my Dad's so happy I'm marrying someone like him. I didn't want to disappoint him. I'm so mad at myself I couldn't tell him the truth. I don't know how to be.

THE DRUNKEN CITY
Adam Bock

Dramatic
Marnie, twenties

> *Marnie is talking to a guy she just met. They have wandered into*
> *a church and she realizes she has doubts about her impending*
> *marriage.*

MARNIE: It's gonna be a gorgeous wedding. I'm gonna wear my Mom's wedding dress
>> it's from 1910 and her Mom wore it
>> and her mom's mom wore it
>> and it's satin with inlaid pearls, well not inlaid pearls, that's not the word I'm, and I remember when I was a tiny girl I remember thinking "I gonna wear that dress" because it's the most, it's gorgeous and I'm gonna get to be looked at, I'm gonna,
>> Gary was just a prop. He was. He was just
>> And I knew he wanted me to say yes, so I did. I just
>> I kept lying
>> And then, worse, Frank, he suddenly he he changed on me.
>> He started acting like a husband. How he thinks a husband is, the world's dangerous and he has to protect me and that means I have to listen to him and he's gonna tell me what to do and I'm gonna have to act like he tells me. He's gonna be like his Dad. But his Mom's this little mousy woman who never says Boo. And I'm not gonna be her.
>> Uh uh.
>> But I just don't know what to say to Gary.
>> I want to tell him the truth. I do.
>> It's good you brought me here. I'm gonna need some help doing all this. Will you wait for me?
>> I'm gonna go sit and be quiet for a minute. You're so sweet. I wish I'd met you before I met Gary.
> *(She goes offstage to the altar.)*

EARTHQUAKE CHICA

Anne García-Romero

Dramatic
Esmeralda, twenties

> *Esmeralda is talking to her boyfriend about everything in her life which makes her unhappy. She is very depressed.*

ESMERALDA: You have no idea, Sam. I wanna finish things. I can't. I see my sister the physicist and I feel crazy. I think of my father and I wanna run. And then my heart starts pumping. And I can't breathe. And my feet feel like lead. And my stomach fills with glass. And my chest is like a lump of charcoal. And my hair and eye lashes start to fall out. It's not enjoyable. I have to keep moving. I have to.

   . . . But if I stop for too long the empty lonely silence descends and I have no way out. Before booze and boys were the great escape . . . but I don't want that anymore . . . so I have to keep moving. If I don't, my mind starts to earthquake. Starts to move and shift and get destructive. So I'm earthquake *chica* in a way, inside my head, I guess.

   . . . Okay maybe but now you're going back to prison law firm land and I'm going off to this awesome travel world job and yeah I'm excited but like what if I can't stand it and the office smells like toxic chemicals and the travel people are horrible and I won't have you there to talk to and oh god . . . my breath . . . and then . . .

   . . . And then but I'll be all alone. And I hate my tiny apartment. I lie in bed and I hear my nutcase neighbor screaming at his Siamese cat or playing electric bass at midnight and I think what's the point? Why live another day? I mean why have all this craziness inside my head? Oh god . . . my breath.

   . . . No really, what's the point? If I'm an earthquake and I'm so destructive, why keep being here on this planet? Why not just leave forever? Everyone's left me. I'm not helping anyone apparently. I'm not really good at anything. I can't finish jobs . . . I can't even have relationships. Really, why be here? Why not just leave for good . . . who really cares anyway?

. . . You say you care but do you really? I don't think so. I mean you can't stand to be with me so much that you're going back to that horrible job in that far away land where large bellied secretaries roam. And then you're gone just like everyone else in my life. You don't care really. No one does. But that's OK. I can just leave this planet and no one will care. I mean I lie in bed and I fantasize about how I'd do it. Pills? Razor blades? Rope? And I think maybe. Why not? Who'd care really?

EAT THE RUNT
Avery Crozier

Seriocomic
Merritt, thirties

> *In "Eat the Runt" the audience chooses which roles the actors will play during the performance. In the performance I saw Merritt was played by a woman so I have included this monologue in this book; but the role could just as easily be played by a man. Here, she/he is interviewing for a job at a museum.*

MERRITT: It's ridiculous. The opposite of survival of the fittest. If the best person doesn't get the job, where are we all — as a species — headed? . . . Oh, I'm not talking about myself. It's a pervasive problem, bigger than affirmative action, really. I don't wanna sound cold-hearted, but we as a society spend too much time guarding the rights of the unfit. And I'm not saying they should have any fewer rights than anyone else, but they certainly shouldn't have *more*. . . . But see, there's an example. You'll judge me partly on my understanding of your joke, the cultural recognition of Ayn Rand's philosophy in the novel and the movie. My education and ability give me an advantage rather than some unrelated factor like ethnicity. . . . Think of all the regulations we have in this country to pro-tect stupid people. To ensure that they survive, reproduce, and con-tribute — disastrously — to the gene pool. The closest we've come to this kind of genetic crisis is the nineteenth century's preservation of hemophilia in the royal families of Europe. . . . Why put big warning labels on cigarettes and let so-called victims sue tobacco companies? If they're dumb enough to start smoking, let them die. We don't need their dopey, suicidal genes. Better yet, increase the nicotine and carcinogens in cigarettes to hook them quicker and kill them before they have a chance to reproduce. . . . It's just practical for the species. When my dog had pup-pies, she ate the runt. Why can't we have that much sense?

ELLIOT, A SOLDIER'S FUGUE
Quiara Alegría Hudes

Dramatic
Ginny, twenties

Ginny talks about how she loves gardening.

Ginny is in the garden.

GINNY: The garden is twenty-five years old. It used to be abandoned. There was glass everywhere. Right here, it was a stripped-down school bus. Here, a big big pile of old tires. I bought it for one dollar. A pretty good deal. Only a few months after I came back from Vietnam. I told myself, you've got to *do* something. So I bought it. I went and got a ton of dirt from Sears. Dirt is expensive! I said, when I'm done with this, it's going to be a spitting image of Puerto Rico. Of Arecibo. It's pretty close. You can see electric wires dangling like right there and there. But I call that "native Philadelphia vines." If you look real close, through the heliconia you see anti-theft bars on my window.

    Green things, you let them grow wild. Don't try to control them. Like people, listen to them, let them do their own thing. You give them a little guidance on the way. My father was a mean bastard. The first time I remember him touching me, it was to whack me with a shoe. He used to whack my head with a wooden spoon every time I cursed. I still have a bump on my head from that. Ooh, I hated him. But I was mesmerized to see him with his plants. He became a saint if you put a flower in his hand. Secrets, when things grow at night. Phases of the moon. He didn't need a computer, he had it all in his brain "I got no use for that." That was his thing. "I got no use for church." "I got no use for a phone." "I got no use for children." He had use for a flower.

35

There are certain plants you only plant at night. Orchids. Plants with provocative shapes. Plants you want to touch. Sexy plants. My garden is so sexy. If I was young, I'd bring all the guys here. The weirdest things get my juices going. I sit out here at night, imagine romances in the spaces between banana leaves. See myself as a teenager, in Puerto Rico, a whole different body on these bones. I'm with a boygriend, covered in dirt.

When I was a nurse in the Army Nurse Corps, they brought men in by the loads. The evacuation hospital. The things you see. Scratched corneas all the way to. A guy with the back of his body torn off. You get the man on the cot, he's screaming. There's men screaming all around. Always the same thing, calling out for his mother, his wife, girlfriend. First thing, before anything else, I would make eye contact. I always looked them in the eye, like to say, hey, it's just you and me. Touch his face like I was his wife. Don't look at his wound, look at him like he's the man of my dreams. Just for one tiny second. Then, it's down to business. Try to keep that heart going, that breath pumping in and out, keep that blood inside the tissue. Sometimes I was very attracted to the men I worked on. A tenderness would sweep through me. Right before dying, your body goes into shock. Pretty much a serious case of the shakes. If I saw a man like that, I thought, would he like one last kiss? One last hand on his ass? Give him a good going away party.

Just things in my mind. Not things you act on.

With George, though. We had a great time when he was in the evacuation hospital. I stitched his leg up like a quilt and we stayed up all night smoking joints. Everyone in the hospital was passed out asleep. The first time George got up and walked to me. I took his head in my right hand and I kissed him so hard. That kiss was the best feeling in my body. Ooh. You see so much death, then someone's lips touches yours and you go on vacation for one small second.

Gardening is like boxing. It's like those days in Vietnam. The wins versus the losses. Ninety percent of it is failures but the triumphs? When Elliot left for Iraq, I went crazy with the planting. Begonias, ferns, trees. A seed is a contract with the future. It's saying, I know something better will happen tomorrow. I planted bearded irises next to palms. I planted tulips with a border of cacti. All the things the book tells you, "Don't ever plant these together." "Guide to Proper Gardening." Well I got on my knees and planted them side by side. I'm like, you have to throw all preconceived notions out the window. You have to plant wild. When your son goes to war, you plant every goddamn seed you can find. It doesn't matter what the seed is. So long as it grows. I plant like I want and to hell with the consequences. I planted a hundred clematis vines by the kitchen window, and next thing I know sage is growing there. The tomato vines gave me beautiful tomatoes. The bamboo shot from the ground. And the heliconia! *(She retrieves a heliconia leaf.)* Each leaf is actually a cup. It collects the rainwater. So any weary traveler can stop and take a drink.

FALL FORWARD
Daniel Reitz

Dramatic
Woman 1, twenties to thirties

The speaker is a woman of lapsed faith. She is in a church and is talking to a man about what being here engenders in her.

WOMAN 1: *(Indicates the church.)* Do you believe in all this?

. . . I mean, for instance — Italy. The churches. Magnificent tranquil places. There's this particular church in Venice . . . off the beaten path. You walk in, on your way, say, to breakfast, St. Mark's Square, somewhere, there's a Rubens Madonna. Right there. *That's* Italy. My husband and I saw many a church in our time. *(Pause.)* But I don't believe in prayer because I don't believe in magic. And I will not pray to what I have no faith in. Nor do I believe things happen for a reason. Well, I believe *some* things happen for a reason. Not a rational reason, maybe. The senseless events that happen for a logic known only to those who are committed to making them happen. *(Pause.)*

. . . Should you? *(Pause.)* "In the midst of life we are in death." That's what the Episcopalians say at the graveside. I'm not an Episcopalian. I'm a lapsed you-name-it.

. . . Is there a better place for a lapsed you-name-it than a church?

. . . I used to think, in the hierarchy of demise, there is deliberate death by someone else's hand, death by accident, and then death by nature. I used to think, if I thought much about it at all, and I didn't really, but if I did, I thought that the pain of losing someone would be less if it were *not* wrought by human hands. Second best, or worst, was the plane that goes down because they didn't see the engine trouble. And the least if it were, say, an earthquake. Nature always gets a pass because, well, it's nature. And planes are planes. It's humans we can't forgive.

FOOD FOR FISH
Adam Szymkowicz

Dramatic
Sylvia, twenties

Sylvia is talking to Bobbie, her boyfriend, about how she is scared to fall in love.

SYLVIA: Go ahead and stop me then. *(Silence.)* What, you can't? No, you can't stop me now, can you? The night is blank and the streets are empty. I pick a direction at random and begin running. I feel like I am running through water. My legs don't move like I tell them. My brain is mush holding on to a single thought — that I must find him. I run and I run and the air is water and my brain is melting. I am about to give up. I can't see anything, anyone, anywhere. And then he is there. Where were you? No, I'm sorry. Don't go. Shit! I'm so stupid. Wait for me. He walks more slowly this time. As if he's waiting for me. But he still doesn't look in my direction or seem to see me in his periphery. I stare at him as we walk along, oblivious to the night, the neighborhood, to everything. Then we are standing in front of a brownstone. Then we are in the hall. Then we are in his apartment or what I assume is his apartment. How can I explain that I'm not afraid? Yes, it is dangerous, but not any more dangerous than falling in love. When it comes down to it, what it really does is make a piece of metal move very quickly. It doesn't ever get to the root of things. It just takes care of the surface problem — if that's what it's for, that is. I don't ask what it's there for. But let me be clear I'm not afraid. I am more afraid of what he is writing. I am afraid of his command of language, his diction, the way the verbs might rub up against my palate or jam themselves, get stuck in my throat. I am afraid I might like it too much, get used to it. Or maybe instead it's the opposite: I am afraid of disappointment. I am afraid of who I think he is and more afraid he isn't. Then he speaks to me for the first time, although he looks away from me as if anyone in the room might catch his voice and latch onto it and find meaning in it and, if it happened to be me, well so be it. He says: "If you stay here, I will hold you all night long." So I do.

FUCK TORI AMOS
Caitlyn Montanye Parrish

Dramatic
Audrey, twenties

> *Audrey is talking to Geoff about her philosophy of life, which is to*
> *trust no one and never let anyone fuck you over.*

AUDREY: Do you . . . would you say you really like other people?
   . . . I don't like people my age. They all seem tired. It makes
sense, though. High school is exhausting. People suck. What the
hell, Geoff? Dad's freaking out at me because of what, exactly? I wish
I could . . . I don't know. I remember in preschool there was an elec-
tion between pretzels for snack time and cheese-it's for snack time.
And I voted for pretzels and lost, but this other kid got a bunch of
people that didn't care to vote for cheese-its, and they won, even
though pretzels are clearly the superior snack food. That's not really
. . . there's something that's supposed to work in the world but it's
broken. Sorry, we were talking about you.
   . . . Never let people fuck you around. Never let Dad win just
'cause he's louder. And never. Never ever let a girl convince you that
you, for any reason, ever have to listen to Tori Amos. If she says
you'll like it she's a filthy little bitch whore of a liar. The day I real-
ized all good had been sucked from music was the day I heard her
cover of "Smells Like Teen Spirit." Something in me shriveled and
died that I can never get back. It's like a little raisin that lives in my
lungs. Ooh, look at me. I play piano and I have red hair. I was
raped, I must be talented.

GIFTBOX
Francine Volpe

Dramatic
A, twenties

A is talking about why she gave up acting.

A: Just let me say one thing. I was an artist. You know that I was an artist. I wanted to act. You know that I studied. I went to that scene study class. I had a vocal coach. You know I had that coach. I wanted it. But I couldn't get a break. Nobody wanted to see me.

Did you know I was about to get signed? Big agency. About to sign me. Big big agency. Big agency. Just when I found out I was pregnant.

I didn't know how I felt about it all. No really. But. So I went to the movies. I went and saw a movie. And in the movie there was a family. That made all the wrong choices. And their bad choices led to misery. Just . . . misery. And in the end they commit suicide. They tie bags over their heads. And we see their distorted faces like masks.

I thought to myself. I don't ever have to act. Not ever again. To . . . For what? To participate in that? To participate in *that.* So that everyone can sit and watch the people die. Watching them living and dying . . . at the same time.

I just. Felt what was important. And then it was clear. What was important was clear to me. I hope that you have that moment. I do. I don't want you to be so confused. I don't. And I love you. And I know. In the end. All this acting out. All this. It's because that's really all you want to hear from me.

GIFTBOX
Francine Volpe

Dramatic
C, twenties

> *C assures another woman that she is not sleeping with her boy-friend and tells her why she never made it as an actress.*

C: You're a liar.

... YOU ARE MAKING ME SICK. I didn't sleep with your boyfriend ok he's my friend he's my friend. And you are not my friend. I had to ask a stranger to drive me to a clinic and I couldn't call you because I knew what I'd get from you. I know you. You see I know you. You'd rather make yourself feel righteous than help me. Than help me. Than help. You want to know why you can't act? Because you're not capable of ever imagining yourself as someone else. You act like good fortune is some kind of reward for good behavior but the world doesn't work like that. The world is inexplicable, I know it. I know it because I've seen it.

But you never asked me. You never asked me where I was going. Or where I'd been. Or what I'd seen. You cut yourself off. You've cut yourself off from it.

... But the world ... the world is *vast*. And it is filled with all the people you will never see. And all that you will never be ... So how many abortions have you had? Think. How many abortions have you had?

GOD'S EAR
Jenny Schwartz

Dramatic
Mel, thirties

Mel tells her husband what he means to her.

MEL: And then we'll kiss.
    And then I'll scratch your back.

    Higher.
    A little higher.
    There.
    Right there.

    And then you'll hold me.
    And protect me.
    And I'll forgive you.
    And you'll understand me.

    And I'll never stop loving you.
    And you won't ever think of leaving me.
    And I'll laugh at all your jokes.
    And you'll never disappoint me.

    And you'll swoop down and save the day.
    And I'll bend over backwards and light up the room.

    And we'll thank God.
    And God will bless America.
    And with God as our witness, we'll never be starving again.

    And the fog will lift.
    And we'll see eye to eye.

And the cows will come home.
And we'll dance cheek to cheek.

And we'll face the music.
And smell the coffee.
And know where to turn.
And which end is up.

And the dogs will stop biting.
And the bees will stop stinging.
And this too shall pass.
And all good things.

And we'll make love.
The old-fashioned way.
Blind-folded.
With one hand tied behind our back.

And Hell will be freezing.
And pigs will be flying.
And Rome will be built.
And water will be wine.

And truth will be told.
And needs will be met.
And boys will be boys.
And enough will be enough.

And we'll cross that bridge.
And bridge that gap.
And bear that cross.
And cross that "t".

And part that sea.
And act that part.
And turn that leaf.
And turn that cheek.

And speak our minds.
And mind our manners.
And clear our heads.
And right our wrongs.

And count our blessings.
And count our chickens.
And pick our battles.
And eat our words.

And take it slow.
And make it last.
And have it made.
And make it fast.

And take it back.
And see it through.
And see the light.
And raise the roof.

And make the most.
And make the best.
And work it out.
And mend the fence.

And wait it out.
And play it down.
And live it up.
And paint the town.

And take care.
And eat right.
And sleep well.
And stay calm.

And have fun.
And have faith.

And face facts.
And move on.

And own up.
And come clean.
And start fresh.
And take charge.

And stand tall.
And save face.
And steer clear.
And live large.

And then we'll kick up our heels.
And have it both ways.
And take a deep breath.
And take it like men.

And sit back.
Relax.

And ride off into the horse-shit.

For richer, for poorer.
In sickness and in health.
And the fat lady will sing.
With bells on.

GOD'S EAR

Jenny Schwartz

Seriocomic
Lenora, thirties

> *Lenora is talking to a guy she has just met in a bar. She does both*
> *roles in what in her experience has been a typical first encounter*
> *between a man and a woman.*

LENORA: You can tell a lot about a man by his pulse.

My ex, for instance, you can tell by his pulse, that a) he's dehydrated, and b) he's sick and twisted and c) he doesn't want to be tied down.

And I'm like, "No problem. Neither do I."

And so I buy him a watch.

Gold-plated.

And I get it engraved.

Genuine leather.

And he's like, "Is it water-proof?"

And I'm like, "It's engraved."

And he's like, "Is it water-proof?"

And I'm like, "It's engraved."

And he's like, "Is it water-proof?"

And I'm like, "It's engraved."

And he's like, "A figure eight?"

And I'm like, "An infinity sign."

And he's like, "A figure eight?"

And I'm like, "An infinity sign."

And he's like, "A figure eight?"

And I'm like, "An infinity sign."

And he's like, "Because time is infinite?"

And I'm like, "Because love is infinite."

And he's like, "I told you from the start . . ."

And I'm like, "Who is that in the background?"

And he's like, "Francine."

And I'm like, "My cousin?"

And he's like, "She's hot."

And I'm like, "I'm pregnant."

And he's like, "Get rid of it."

And I'm like, "I'm 35."

And he's like, "You're 39."

And I'm like, "I'm 35."

And he's like, "You're 39."

And I'm like, "I'm 35."

And he's like, "You're a train wreck."

And I'm like, "I need you in my life."

And he's like: "You're damaged goods."

And I'm like: "I need you in my life."

And he's like: "You wanna have a three-way?"

And I'm like: "Isn't that incest?"

And he's like: "Forget it."

And so I go over.

And I ring the bell.

And I know they're in there.

And I'm like, "Francine, how can you do this to me, Francine?"

And he's like, "Francine can't help it if she's hot. Can you, Francine?"

And she's like, "No, not really, no."

And I'm like, "Haven't you ever heard of loyalty?"

And they're like, "Haven't you ever heard of fetal alcohol syndrome?"

And I'm like, "I'm not even going to dignify that with a response."

GREAT FALLS
Lee Blessing

Dramatic
Bitch, sixteen

"Bitch" is on a cross-country road trip with her stepfather. Here she tells him about the night she lost her virginity, which has led to her pregnancy.

BITCH: *(A beat.)* I was a virgin 'til a little while ago. I mean, I had a boyfriend. We messed around and everything like everybody else. We did a lot of stuff, mostly just to get him off. . . . Yes, I do. Anyhow, as virgins go, I was getting more "technical" all the time. Don't know why I was keeping it. Wasn't waiting to be in love or anything. But given my special history, I guess I didn't . . . feel comfortable yet. . . . My boyfriend was totally frustrated. He wouldn't admit it, though. He was being sensitive, you know? I was getting pretty good at oral, but — . . . *But* it was obvious I was going to lose him if I didn't put out pretty soon, so — . . . I didn't know how I was going to be the first time. Since I was so "special". Since Dad had made me so special. I was afraid I'd get all insane and panicky with my boyfriend. So I asked a friend of his instead. . . . Kid we both knew, sort of. In our class, anyway. I told him I wanted to lose it: one-time thing, no biggie. I don't know why I picked him; I didn't like him. Maybe that's why. Anyhow, he said come on over, his folks were out of town. We could drink, smoke, loosen me up a little. Zip-zap, shouldn't take long. *And* he was right. It didn't. Blood on the towel — he *did* put down a towel. Blood all over my thighs. I was so drunk and stoned, I barely remember it. . . . What I do remember is *his* friend. . . . We were in the middle of doing it the second time. He insisted on a second time — even though I hurt, and there was blood all over — because, he said, he was always better the second time. I didn't want to, but he just rolled on top of me and was like, shut the fuck up, I'd get used to it. And he was bigger than me, and I couldn't push him off. So anyhow, in the middle of us doing it again, his friend came in the room. . . . No, he called him up when I was in the bathroom. Said he should come over and "share the booty" — some pirate expression like that. They laughed about it while they took turns holding me down so each one of them could fuck me. The more I fought, the more they laughed. Oh, and his friend teased him for using a condom, so they both went bareback.

GUARDIANS
Peter Morris

Dramatic
American Girl, late teens to early twenties

> *Speaker is a U.S. soldier. Here she talks about her cousin, a prison guard back in the U.S. who got himself thrown into prison with the same inmates he used to guard for forcing a female living in a school bus to perform oral sex on him.*

AMERICAN GIRL: I guess I'm lucky I'm not directin' traffic. That's what most of us was doing. But prison guard? God *damn*. Back at home, that's *low*. Lower'n whale shit. Scum of the earth. Lookit. I had a cousin, name was Skeeter, which should tell ya something about what kinda PWT oxycontin-suckin' lowlife hillbilly *buttmunch* this guy was. Skeeter Dunkle. He worked at the state facility, and far as I could tell, his job was mainly helping people on the inside break the law *more,* takin' twenny dollars here, twenny dollars there, arrange for them to get breaks, smugglin' a bag a weed and what-all.

And he was kinda slow. And also kinda mean. And he wasn't real good looking neither: kinda guy they gotta tie a porkchop 'round his neck to get the dog to play with 'im. So I guess that's why one night, Skeeter goes over, and — 'kay, there's this family up near where he lived, who are livin' in a schoolbus. They don't drive it noplace — it's up on cinderblocks anyhow — they just live in it. I mean, it's got curtains and all. I can't remember that lady's name, but she's common-law-married and they got a kid — like, the people almost make Skeeter look good. So one night he turns up 'round eleven, drags this lady outta the schoolbus and flashes some kinda phony badge, I guess corrections officers got a badge too, and then he's got — I mean, can you believe what a dipshit this guy is? — he's got a *flare* gun pointed at her head, and gives her some fuckin' story about how the schoolbus is parked illegally but he's gonna look the other way if she just, y'know . . . she puts his thing in her mouth. So she does.

But here's the point of the story, is, she tells the cops, so good ole Skeeter gets picked up, shipped off, and locked up, in the zack-same prison he useta guard. And the other guards? They know him. But they don't *wanna* know him. They just wanna feed him to the animals. American Gladiator style. And the animals in Skeeter's cage? Well, they all know him too, but they ain't thinkin' 'bout the times he did 'em favors. They're thinkin' about the times he used a billyclub. He's the enemy. So the first thing they done is they cut him with a shiv, straight across the belly, like that — *(She mimes slicing a knife straight across her stomach.)*

— so if he *does* get transferred to a different prison? Then all his new buddies gonna read that like a sign, and know what he is.

GUARDIANS
Peter Morris

Dramatic
American Girl, late teens to early twenties

> *Speaker was a prison guard in Iraq, now in prison for abuse of
> Iraqi prisoners. Here, she tells her side of the story.*

AMERICAN GIRL: It's easier for you to care about a dumb Eye-raqi
sumbitch than it is to care about me an my fellow soldiers. 'Cause
what we do, what I do, what I get *made* to do, makes y'all feel guilty.
Makes ya feel bad.

Not just what we do in Eye-Raq. I'm talking 'bout the whole
U.S. Army here. What we do all across the GD planet, just for you.
Air Force takes the sky and the Navy takes the water. The Corps got
the Halls a Montezuma and the Shores a Tripoli covered, which
sounds like a pussy job to me, no matter what they want ya to
believe. But the U.S. Army? We go everyplace else. Which means
anywhere on the globe where shit gets spilled, and they need a girl
with a mop. To mop the shit up. Before it oozes down to the bot-
tom of your easy chair. You know that. And that's why you feel bad.

But how I see it? Me and that brown person on the floor, we're
the same, almost. We both had a run of bad luck. Was he in the
wrong place at the wrong time? Maybe he don't have no useful
information? Well. Tough Titty, Miss Kitty. He's still locked up in
jail, we still gonna treat him like shit, just 'cause he happened to be
in the wrong place in Baghdad that particular day. Same as me.

But when I get shipped back here, everybody's sayin: "That,
uh, even if there *were* orders from above — which we got no evi-
dence that there was, *of course* — it is no defense to say she was just
following orders." And what can I say to that? 'Cept: Hey dumbass,
listen up. I'm *in* the Army, I work 'longside these people, I am one
a them, and trust me: They're good people but they ain't smart

enough to organize a peanut-butter-and-jelly *sandwich*. I love 'em but man, these people could fuck up a baked potato. And now, Senator, you want 'em making their own decisions about, about — what's Right and what's Wrong?

Which, I might note, is not a rule those boys lay down on themselves. Fuck up when you're me, they sell you down the river, baby. But fuck up when you're the Preznit? Two weeks later and who remembers?

So. Here I am now, down the river. And what'm I gonna do about it?

Sit here and cry?

You know: I *could* do that. But I tole ya. I know this better'n most. Cryin' for y'all's a great way to get you to start thinking: Who the fuck is this person and why should I care?

THE HOPPER COLLECTION

Mat Smart

Dramatic
Marjorie, twenties to thirties

*Marjorie is looking at and commenting on a book of paintings by
Edward Hopper.*

MARJORIE: Don't you love the way he titles things. *Chair Car. Chair Car.*
Straight to it. Goose bumps. Forgive my little indulgence here.
Danny-boy hates this game. But I love love love it. I have a whole
wardrobe.

Oh! Look, look, look! Before the sun goes down. We don't have
much light left. See those windows above? They're diffused of
course — so the exposure doesn't damage the canvas as much as it
would — but I think it looks so much better in the natural light —
rather than the artificial. So much better. The difference really is . . .
I was going to say night and day, but that's sort of . . . well, let us
take a moment to enjoy the last of the natural light on the Hopper.

. . . It's funny. The light — no matter what you try to do to it
to make it less harmful — to diffuse it — it still, very slowly, is ruin-
ing the painting. Destroying it. But what is the alternative? To keep
it in the dark? Make an airtight and airless case for you — for it —
I mean for it . . . *(Pause.)*

. . . See there, the light coming in. Some purples maybe. It
almost starts to glow. Oh, you picked a good time. Those next few
minutes are probably the best all day.

. . . I get dozens and dozens of requests and calls — but these
people are all so sterile sounding — so academic. And I should only
want to share this with those people who *appreciate* it the same way
I do . . . and I can't tell you how much I *appreciated* your letter. I

assumed young people today had . . . well, with the way they dress and talk and the music and guns and how everything is Sex Sex Sex — I had grown to think true love was . . . But then your letter appears . . . So you haven't seen . . . Sarah in two years?

HUNTING AND GATHERING

Brooke Berman

Dramatic
Bess, twenties

Bess, a college student, talks about how she learned to shoot a gun.

BESS: All the girls are learning to shoot. We're also playing poker, but I think that shooting is the really essential thing. We practice on a video game called Big Buck Hunter. We love relaxing into our lower bodies, waiting for the moment — the one right before the kill. "See it, then shoot it." This guy named Steve showed me how to hold the gun right up next to my face, between the torso and the arm, higher up, like a violin. Remember when I learned to play violin in the fifth grade? Remember how I sucked? Well, I do not suck at Buck Hunter. I have a natural killers' instinct, which I think will help me immeasurably as I work my way through the Western European canon, AKA my college career. Speaking of the which, I'm taking this awesome class called "Essential Cinema of New York: Cassavetes, Scorsese, Allen and Lee." I'm either writing my midterm on "She's Gotta Have It" or else, "Manhattan." Did you guys see that one in the theaters? It's this really cool old black and white movie about when New York was intellectual and people still lived uptown. Spike Lee's movie is also black and white, and people also live uptown, but it's different. Anyway. Later Skaters — Bess.

HUNTING AND GATHERING

Brooke Berman

Dramatic
Ruth, twenties

Ruth is stalking the perfect apartment.

RUTH: Stalking the apartment. I see the apartment. I have identified and looked at it. I have turned in an application. And now, using the Buck Hunter stance, I stand across the street. Every night until they decide. Watching to see what happens, who comes and goes, whether they look nice, whether it feels safe and whether or not this is a place I could belong. I ask, do I feel at home? In the presence of the building, do I feel any instinctual clue? A "homing" device? Can I place my energy into the building from across the street and start to bond with it even before the paperwork has gone through? And then, based on this energetic bond, will the landlord be persuaded to ignore my tax returns and the word "self employed" and pay attention instead to the subtle way in which I already belong in his building?

I pretend to be the girl in the dive bar. The one who moves through life as if it's a straight line. The one who can keep her eye on the target and pursue what she wants without fear. For that girl, there is no ambivalence. No theory. No gray area. Just black. And white. A clear path home.

IN OUR NAME
Elena Hartwell

Dramatic
Woman, about forty

> *Speaker is a mother of a son serving in Iraq, talking to someone*
> *who is against the war.*

WOMAN: We're in it now that's for sure. It's going to be a long time before
we bring all our boys
    . . . and our girls. Before we bring our children home. I got this
letter from my son today. The army is running out of new recruits,
they've lowered their standards. No, that's not right. They haven't
lowered, they have just modified them. Rolled with the punches.
That's what you have to do sometimes. Go with what you've got.
My son was accepted this time around. He ships out in a month.
Straight to Iraq. Straight into combat. He says he'll stick it out until
we win. And we have to win before we bring our children home,
right? Otherwise, what was it all for? We can't leave until we win.
My son understands that I taught him that. It's because of me that
he's going over there. He's going in my name. I know it's the right
thing. I know it's the right thing. We have to stay until we win. I
don't know why people like you can't see that.

IN THE SHADOW OF MY SON

Nadine Bernard

Dramatic
Tristyn, twenties to thirties

> *Tristyn had her first baby six months ago and has been suffering
> from post-partum depression, but she's really good at putting on a
> happy face and hiding it. Here, she shares with the audience the
> truth about how she really feels.*

TRISTYN: *(Mocking herself.)* "She's got a healthy appetite." . . .
(Takes off her mask.)

    Remember how I used to be, how I used to talk? I'm counting
on you, cause it's slipping away. I can't remember.
(With sudden vigor which lasts a moment, as she sits on the cube.)

    I used to sit like this, right, with my legs under me or stretched
out like this — young and fun loving. I'm a "Mom," now you say.
I'm simply more mature, more tired and more mature. Six months
and I grew up, you say, got that maternal poise . . . *(Moves to the
ground, leaning on cube.)* I used to reach out and talk. Lay on my
back on the grass, the cordless in my hands, and tell with honesty
all the secrets in my heart. But what is a girlfriend now? Someone
to compare notes with about diapers and baby food? Who wants to
hear the other stuff? A gorgeous guy sitting across from us on the
bus, my favorite jeans (which don't fit now) ripped in the crotch. All
the things that used to make me giggle and feel young. Who wants
to hear? That's selfish of me now. I'm a mother now. Who wants to
hear? So my friends are slipping away too. There's a gauze between
me and the rest of the world.
*(Baby cries again. Tristyn is on the ground and can't muster enough
motivation to go and get her baby. The next passage is very gut level,
deep and rooted.)*

I hear my child cry, and I feel the muffled cries inside myself. The cries I used to share with lovers and friends. But the cries of a new mother are so vivid and deep and wrenching, like the wailing of a mourner. I was ripped open during childbirth. I was an open vessel to all the things of this earth. . . . The wails inside me are huge. And they'll eat me up for months to come as they sit stagnant and unheard. Because all "They" want to hear are the smiles.

JOY
John Fisher

Seriocomic
Jane, twenties

Jane is talking with a group of friends about the gay members of her family.

JANE: My uncle practically owns this place. The museum board ran out of money half-way through construction and my uncle's like this sleazy loan-shark type and he put up the rest of the money because he's trying to clean up his name in this town because the police busted him a few months ago sucking off a male hustler in the toilet of the Union Square Garage. And Herb Caen wrote that whole column about it. My uncle told me to bring Christian along because he's in lust with him. He lusts after all my boyfriends. *(To Gabe.)* You have got a great voice, man. *(To Darryl.)* Yours is alright. *(To the world.)* I love old shit: Cole Porter, Gershwin — George and Ira. My mother listens to it. She lives in West Hollywood. My father lives in Bel Aire. But he's a total asshole. He actually went through this whole youth thing shit and became a fag when he was like forty years old. Now he cruises bars and picks up teenagers and listens to Aretha Franklin and does coke and he is totally old looking and pathetic. He used to work for Paramount until he blew this whole deal with Kate Moss to make her first movie because she decided he was too much of a creepy fag and she couldn't handle it so she told him to fuck off! Kate hates fags. Except Calvin Klein of course. But she's totally fat anyway. They've been keeping it a big secret and now they're sending her to a farm. She's a fucking cow. Moo. *(And she assumes a Kate Moss pose which she holds then acts as if she is being attacked by bats. Slowly she recovers.)*

LOVE-LIES-BLEEDING
Don DeLillo

Dramatic
Toinette, thirties

> *Toinette is talking to an ex-boyfriend about why her current guy is better for her than he was.*

TOINETTE: *(Strong male voice.)* stand clear of the closing doors, please. *(A pause indicating a passage of time. Light changes as sunset approaches. Alex sits close to her now.)* I was the only person you talked to, ever, about anything that mattered. Now I talk to Sean. He's living somewhere in Pennsylvania. You're not interested in this. Teaching at a private academy for rich kids who deal drugs. He calls me up, all hours. How angry does it make you, knowing that he and I talk? You're ready to rip me apart. I'll tell him that. There's no moment too fleeting for Sean. He wants to hear everything. The little cookbook of human motive. Your rages, my betrayals. Or lack of motive. Unknown motive. The near nightly drama of Alex murderously brooding. You brooded on things. You blamed me for things. You developed elaborate brooding theories. You blamed me for the art world, everything and everybody in it. Sean listens. He calls me up and listens. I withhold things from him. I make him beg a little. The time you rode the Staten Island Ferry, back and forth, all day and into the night, for how many days straight, coming home to do some coke — ten days, maybe twelve.

  . . . We don't talk often but we talk. Sean and I. It's talk on the level of heartbreak TV. We talk because you're rooted in our lives. We're too weak to let you go, or too empty. Let's face it, you wouldn't be worth the time otherwise. I'm not sure how it works but men who don't know themselves have a power over others, those who try miserably to understand. I owe him something, your son. I owe him roughly half a life.

MARVELOUS SHRINE
Leslie Bramm

Dramatic
Bobbie, about forty

Bobbie talks about the death of her son in Iraq.

BOBBIE: His presence all over the house. I smell his clothes. See his hair in a brush. His voice on the machine. All these pieces of my son. 18 hours! That's how long my son fought to stay alive. That's how long he lay twisted and broken. That fragile body, mangled, burnt! 18 hours, in his pain, almost a full day, and I wasn't there. I wasn't there to hold his hands. Five hundred miles from home, where was I? And, where are you Peter? Where do you call from? You go without me? Without telling me? Without taking me? As soon as I hear the phone ring, I know it's you, and I know why. For a moment everything just hangs there, in the air. If I don't answer . . . If . . . The machine picks up your voice . . . and now my son is dead. "I regret to inform you," is what you said? I play it over and over. "I regret . . . I regret . . . I regret" . . . At his funeral a Major and three other Marines . . . "You must be mistaken my son hasn't even shipped out yet. There must be some-kind of . . . You've cremated my son? This is a mistake." The Major has dry spit in the corner of his mouth. It looks like Tom's toothpaste. He says my son's name. I think he's talking about you at first. I'm relieved. Then he repeats it, to make sure I hear. My son's death, simple as your phone call. Gritty and sweet, like the taste of toothpaste. He has dog tags in his hand. He has a box. Smaller than a shoe box . . . Dust . . . I can hold him in one hand. Not since he was a baby . . . "No. No, it's not possible," I tell him. If my son had died . . . if my son was dying, don't you think I'd be there? Wouldn't his mother be there for him? Besides, he never called me back. He was supposed to call me back. I was waiting for that call . . . The Major apologizes, again. After a while

I don't even hear the words. I watch his mouth. I watch the spit . . .
I watch him trying to wet his lips. They gave me a flag. Neatly
folded . . . I gave them a young man. A perfectly beautiful boy . . .
He burned to death . . . I gave them a boy. They gave me a flag.

MAURITIUS
Theresa Rebeck

Dramatic
Jackie, twenties

> *Jackie has inherited her grandfather's stamp collection, which contains an incredibly rare misprint from Mauritius which may be worth millions. Problem is, her sister Mary, to whom she is talking, thinks the stamp collection is her property.*

JACKIE: My CHARACTER? I have no character. What I have is two tiny tiny slips of paper, so small that they barely exist, and I'm going to take them, and I'm going to stab myself in the chest with a pair of really sharp scissors, and then I'm going to put those two tiny tiny slips of paper inside my body, right where my heart is supposed to be. And then I'm going to grow a pair of wings, big, blue and green scaly wings, not beautiful wings, BUG wings, the kind that move real fast. And then I'm going to go. Somewhere. Where they like tall girls, with bug wings. And then I'm going to lay in the sun and have a margarita.

. . . Yeah, I'll get right on that. 'Cause you know what I read today, on the internet? Something called the Three Skilling Banco got sold about ten years ago, for two and a half *million* dollars. The one penny magenta, some stamp from British Guiana which some zillionaire has in some bank vault somewhere, they think that's worth maybe ten million dollars. Guess what else. Seven years ago a pair of uncancelled one and two penny post off stamps? Went for six million dollars. At auction. Can you believe that? Six. Million. Dollars.

MEN OF STEEL
Qui Nguyen

Dramatic
Camille, twenties

*Camille is talking to her boyfriend, a cop, about her low opinion
of the police, which is why they can't be together anymore.*

CAMILLE: Bobby, when's the last time you had to spend any real time in
a hospital?

. . . When was the last time you had to sit in a waiting room
because one of you cops got all shot up?

. . . When's the last time you knew anyone who died because
of a super?

. . . It's nice that you think that supers are heroes. That's nice.
Real nice. But that shit ain't universal. They're no heroes to us. They
only worry about saving folks in the city or overseas — commercial
areas where they can get photo ops and publicity. They don't give a
shit about us on the fringe.

. . . I'm pissed because every single thug criminal, and lowlife
that once lived over there has come here because they know they
can run freely without interference. Because everyone has gotten so
dependent on heroes, no one is keeping an eye out anymore. Cops
are getting drunk in the middle of their shifts to deal with their girl-
friends and when shit does hit the fan — it's not you who has to
deal with it. It's us. Boys here are getting killed left and right tryin'
to take up the slack that you officers have let go and that the heroes
ignore. So no, Bobby, it's not just a fantasy, it's a bullshit reality that
exists for you, but not for me and that's what makes us different.
That's why we can't be together no more.

NEIGHBORHOOD 3: REQUISITION OF DOOM

Jennifer Haley

Dramatic
Kaitlyn, teens

> *Kaitlyn is talking about a neighborhood boy who got her into an
> on-line video game which uses their neighborhood as a matrix,
> which they must defend against invading aliens.*

KAITLYN: if you divide the Neighborhood
　　along the line of the sewage ditch
　　and fold it in half
　　my room
　　would be right on top of
　　his room
　　so we'd see each other
　　through the ceiling
　　which is kind of how
　　we got together
　　when i needed to escape
　　my mom
　　i could lie in bed
　　and look through the ceiling
　　down at him in his bed
　　looking up through the ceiling
　　and we just sort of
　　knew each other

　　he started playing
　　that game
　　it uploads floorplans
　　from the Neighborhood Association

he showed me a map
of the subdivision
and the wormhole
between our rooms
there are wormholes
all over
the Neighborhood
he said
one of them connects
your imagination
in the game
to what happens
in life
for real

he's got like
obsessed
with finding
that wormhole
he gets stronger with
every level
he draws on
the power
of the Neighborhood
and the power
of the neighborhood
is fear
it's not just
the Cat
vicki
i think you should go through his room

NONE OF THE ABOVE
Jenny Lyn Bader

Dramatic
Jamie, teens

> *Jamie is trying to get Clark, whom her parents have hired to tutor her on the SATs, to give her some money.*

JAMIE: What I *said* doesn't matter. I didn't break the vase. Someone else broke it and I took the blame. So please stop trying to fit me into your little theory of entitlement. Because I do *not* go smashing up precious antiques that is not my idea of a fun time, I have never broken anything in my life.

... It was my boyfriend! Roger Auerbach. And I knew if I told them that he broke it they would make it a rule for me not to see him. And I thought I loved him. So I told them I broke it. That's when they came up with the unique punishment of no allowance for thirteen years.

... No he left me the following week for Sheila Martin. The nonentity who called the other day. The new girl in school. At this point everyone has been at Billington since nursery school and we usually don't take new people after seventh grade? So to have a new girl junior year is like a revelation. All of the men just melted. Also, she's richer than Donald Trump, and she buys him presents, which of course I had to stop doing when my funding was cut off. I have to discuss every potential purchase I make with my mother. So this cramps my style a little bit.

... and if it weren't for the dealing I do? I wouldn't be able to afford the cabs. I'd be in dangerous neighborhoods. Alone. Dependent on the charity of insane adolescent men. And the business itself is pretty dangerous. No one used to care, but the mayor is cracking down on small-timers. We're living in a fascist state.

. . . Would I like to retire? Absolutely. Not just that. I would be a new person.

. . . If you gave me this chance, I would be so dedicated to the SAT, it would blow your mind. Sure I've been paying basic attention, but it would be more. Like the way I'm dedicated to My Life now? I would be dedicated to The Test.

. . . I would develop *study habits*! And I'd be able to afford the basics of growing up in New York. Just the pressure to buy the right brand of sneaker each month is beyond description. Last month if you didn't have top-siders you were nowhere, and now . . .

. . . Not just sneakers. My whole existence. The chaos of this household. My parents . . . like me better when I don't have money. They can relate to me by giving me money. But with a cut, I could manage. All I need is a little freedom. A little spending money.

. . . *(Hesitates.)* Just my usual cut.

. . . Fifteen thousand. I wouldn't want your tuition money I understand that's . . . specifically for your schooling. So you'd still have that, plus 85 thousand. Clark they've cut me off. I know it's hard to believe but I'm like you. I need it.

. . . Okay. I want it. And in a small emotional way you don't understand because you're from somewhere else, I need it.

. . . Think of it like a problem on the test. Clark and Jamie start a business. Clark earns $100,000 plus perks. He wants Jamie to do a good job. Should he pay her: A. $100,000, B. $15,000. C. Five cents, or D. None of the Above?

100 SAINTS YOU SHOULD KNOW

Kate Fodor

Dramatic
Theresa, thirties

> *Theresa is a single mother who is the cleaning woman at a Catholic rectory. Here, she talks to a priest about her desire to find God. Ironically, he has lost his faith.*

> *Note: Matthew's interjections are in brackets.*

THERESA: No. It seemed like such a lie: if this, then that. I had my own hypothesis about the world, which was basically, whatever the fuck happens, happens and we'll probably never know why. Then I got pregnant with Abby when I was in high school and that was pretty much the last straw for my parents. Imagine: you spend all your time thinking up these complicated rules about exactly what will happen under exactly which circumstances, and then your own daughter turns out to be . . . you know, so much not what you expected. *(A beat.)* I'm sorry. Did I say the f-word back there.

[MATTHEW: It's fine. Did your parents throw you out?]

THERESA: They wanted me to go live with my 1,000-year-old grand-mother and finish high school, but I just left. Don't laugh, but for just a little while, I followed the Grateful Dead. Abby and I followed the Dead, and I dropped a lot of acid and she ran around naked with all these other little naked kids and got tangles in her hair. I was looking for something enormous and expansive, but somehow I ended up with this little scrap of a life. I mean, this little nothing thing. You could just vacuum it up with the Dustbuster and it'd be gone. It's nothing at all.

[MATTHEW: You have your daughter. She seems like less of a scrap and more of a handful. If you don't mind my saying so.]

THERESA: I've got nothing for Abby. I mean — I've really got nothing — no stuff, no money, no ideas, no plans. She hears my boyfriend call me names he shouldn't call me when we fight. *(Beat.)* But sometimes lately, since I've been cleaning the rectory, I've been thinking a little bit about God, which is something I really never did before. I mean really never. And then, during your homily, you spoke so beautifully about, you know, humility, and I've been thinking, maybe the state of having nothing and feeling so used up, maybe that's sort of the state God wants me in, not so full of all my ideas about myself and what a rebel I am — but, you know, kind of — ready to listen. Do you think that's true?

PROPERTY
Rosary O'Neill

Dramatic
Monica Falcon, late twenties

Monica is reflecting on the last months of her husband's life.

MONICA: The last year with my husband was a battle I lost every day and
started the next. My husband wanted to die. He couldn't stand getting weak. He was strong before. Raced motorcycles for the thrill.
He didn't want anyone to see that he couldn't walk, so I'd help him
down to his motorcycle, and he'd drive it to the mailbox. The bike
roaring beneath his thin legs. He'd come back to the stairs, exhausted
and sit. And when no one was looking, he'd ease himself up one step
at a time. I smiled from the window — so attentive to what he was
doing, merged with his courage. But finally the world of matter
faded away, and he gave up, and I gave up. I keep thinking of my
husband lying inside his casket. When I went to choose the coffin, I
was so broke I couldn't pay much. Now I'm glad I did. The lids of
the better caskets fit so well. I ran my fingers over the smooth gold
trim. I thought about rain leaking in the casket, and I went and
bought an expensive airtight one. You think when people look at a
casket, they know how much it costs? It's started to rain again.

REGRETS ONLY
Paul Rudnick

Comic
Spencer, a college student

*Spencer tells her parents, who are wealthy New Yorkers, that she is
getting married.*

SPENCER: Alright. Alright. I just have to say something. First of all, I am
so proud to have come of age in an era when women, OK,
American women, OK, privileged American women, OK, privileged American women with great hair, can be all that they can be.
And I am so grateful to all of the pioneering generations of
American feminists, yes, I said the "f" word, who have marched and
battled and sacrificed, just so that I can have a seven-figure salary,
an unlimited expense account and a smokin' hot car. And I take
pride in spending two days every month mentoring inner-city
teenage girls, who I teach to believe in themselves, to believe in their
dreams, and when they go to McDonalds, to at least think about
the salads. And I am dedicating my life to making this world a more
peaceful, a more equitable and a more compassionate place, but
right at this moment I don't really care about any of that bleeding-
heart, do-goody, help-the-helpless horseshit, and do you know why?
   . . . I'm getting married!

REGRETS ONLY
Paul Rudnick

Comic
Tibby, late forties to early fifties

> *Tibby, a wealthy Manhattan socialite, is talking to her daughter,*
> *who is getting married and to Hank, a top lawyer who has been*
> *asked by the President of the United States to help draft an amend-*
> *ment to the Constitution outlawing gay marriage. Little does the*
> *Prez know that Hank is gay.*

TIBBY: Spencer, I love you very much, but first of all, I want you to stop
whining and whimpering. Because the world doesn't owe you a
wedding.

    . . . And Myra, you are going to start cleaning in the corners!

    . . . And Hank, I think you've got a thing or two to learn about
friendship. And respect. And destroying people's lives. So you're
going to call up all of your little buddies, up and down the entire
Eastern seaboard, because they're all going right back to work by
tomorrow morning.

    . . . And Jack, you're going to call your new best friend, the
president of the United States, and you are going to tell him that
you and Spencer are off that amendment.

    . . . Because you're right. We are married. And if that's what gay
people want . . . let 'em learn! Because you know something?
Marriage sucks. Raising a family sucks. And falling in love sucks.
And you know why? Because we're all gonna die. But before I do, I
wanna look gorgeous. I want hair and makeup and dresses and dia-
monds. I wanna make the biggest drag queen of all time say, honey,
too much. I want a world that doesn't exist, that can't exist, a world
where everyone's happy, where everyone's children are perfect,
where everyone's mother is perfect, and where everyone's husband
has fantastic sex with her, pays for everything, tells her she's

beautiful, and leaves. I wanna live inside a Hank Hadley advertisement in the September issue of *Vogue*, the issue that weighs eighteen pounds because it's so packed with lies. That's what I want, and all of you, that's what you're gonna give me. Because I'm a rich white woman, and goddamnit, that's good. We're gonna make it good. And we're gonna have a wedding, because weddings are gorgeous and glorious, and that's how we trick people into getting married. So you just call the President, and you just tell him — I need flowers! I need music! And may God help me, I need cake!

SCHOOL OF THE AMERICAS

José Rivera

Dramatic
Julia, twenties

> *Julia is a Bolivian school teacher. The captured Cuban revolution-*
> *ary Ché Guevara is being held in her school room. She is allowed*
> *by his captors to talk to him. He wants her to embrace the necessity*
> *of revolutionary struggle. She wants him to see the reality of life for*
> *ordinary people just trying to survive.*

JULIA: That's all fine rhetoric, sir — but it's not the reality here. *(Beat.)* My
father gave me, and La Higuera, everything he had. And with almost
no help from the government or the church, we built this "prison" as
you like to call it, using his life savings, so our kids wouldn't go
around thinking — I don't know — the world is flat or sickness
comes from witchcraft — or not know there are actual numbers bigger than "three." Of course some days I have to contend with the
machete-waving grandfather who thinks I'm teaching the children to
be too independent. Or the irate mother who thinks I'm teaching
their daughters to write love letter to their secret boyfriends. Or the
over-protective brother who wants to strangle me for using the word
"sex" in class. And whether I like it or not, I come to work anyway —
though I haven't been paid by the "system" in a year and a half. God!
It'd be so much easier, trust me, to throw my hands up in despair and
leave their education to nature, or chance, or to the insane, old *bru-*
jas of the town! *(Beat.)* Most days I'm lucky to have five kids in here.
The rest are out there trying not to starve to death. Yet through
storms, head lice, or crazy parents — I'm here every day for those five
kids, sir, no questions asked, oh, unless I'm attending one of their
funerals. Which I seem to be doing more and more these days.

A SMALL, MELODRAMATIC STORY
Stephen Belber

Dramatic
O, forties

> *O talks to the audience about the death of her husband, a Gulf War veteran.*

O: *(To audience.)* Keith wants to *know* what happened to my husband. *(Pause.)* Which is the one thing I no longer want to know. *(Beat.)* My husband's name was Burt. Gardner. *(Pause, perhaps a chuckle.)* He was a soldier. Who became a captain, which means he didn't have to fight so much but *did* buy a house in Falls Church. Where I still live. *(Beat.)* Burt and Keith went to college together. U-Maryland. The army paid for them both all the way through; Burt fell in love with the army and made it a career. Keith worked off his debt and grew a ponytail. *(Pause.)* Anyway. *(Beat.)* Anyway, Burt died. Six years ago. He was walking down a street that didn't have streetlights. At three A.M. In a football jersey and flip-flops. And he got hit by a car. *(Pause.)* Burt was a train wreck; a genetic car crash who hated his father, never knew his mother and married a woman who didn't want his kids. *(Pause.)* He lived his life like he didn't really believe it was his, like the thought he'd have to give it back at any moment. And then he did. *(Pause.)* But *Keith* has a theory. Keith says that Burt was always a little odd, but that the oddness turned more into crazy during the early 1990s. Keith thinks Burt died because of PB tablets. Pyridostigmine bromide, the antinerve gas pills they gave out during the first Gulf War. *(Pause.)* Keith sees conspiracy in everything; he probably now despises the Cape Cod Potato Chip company. *(Beat.)* Burt didn't even *go* to the Gulf. At least not with everyone else. He was at a desk in Virginia for most of it, but Keith's convinced that he took these tablets around that time — because they were handing them out like candy — and that somewhere soon after that, on some mission to China or Russia or one of those places he'd go — that Burt breathed in sarin gas instead of soman gas, and that instead of saving his life, the PB combined with the sarin and went straight into his brain stem. And twisted it like a cork. *(Pause.)* Which eventually turned him into the type of guy who takes three A.M. walks in the dark.

I don't know. I didn't even *meet* Burt until a couple years after that war. And he *was* nuts; which made things fun, but . . . *(Beat.)* *My* hunch is that the army *didn't* kill him. That Burt just . . . decided to stop living. Because that's how he was. Because the people in his life didn't trust him — and there weren't enough reasons to stick around. *(Beat . . .) Or . . .* maybe Keith's right. Maybe the answer is in drawer number twelve somewhere, in some sprawling government warehouse. Maybe he can find it. And maybe it *will* change the miserable into lovely.

SMOKE AND MIRRORS
Joseph Goodrich

Dramatic
Anita, twenties to thirties

> *Anita talks about her difficulties with a woman she knows who has a thing for gay guys.*

ANITA: Diane's got this thing for gay guys. As employees. She loves 'em. If you're gay, you can do no wrong. You're not a threat. I mean, you know what Diane looks like, right? She's not exactly, uhhh . . . I don't know — name a movie star . . . The point is, a straight woman, a relatively good-looking straight woman, doesn't have a chance. *(Pause.)* Last Friday, I was showing some of the people in Transport a picture of my son. And everyone's oohing and ahhing over it, because he's really cute if I do say so myself. And I do . . . And Diane — Diane sees us all looking at it and she comes over and she's like, "What's the occasion, folks?" And I show her the photograph — big mistake — and she's like, "Oh! He's so . . . cute!" You know, like how could he be my son if he's so cute. What she's really saying is, "You fucking breeder. You fucking heterosexual." Totally sweet on the surface but totally dismissive underneath. So that's the background . . . Now this morning I just couldn't get the tallies right. Like I said, I tried it by names, numbers, assignments, everything, and it wouldn't add up. And I know it's important, and I know the trucks are waiting, and I know there's a very limited amount of time in which to get the job done. I understand that. And I did finally get it right and everything's OK. But then Diane calls me over to her cubicle and says she wants to have a little talk with me. I say sure and I go over. And we sit down and she's asking me if anything's wrong, am I feeling all right, am I having any problems . . . And I say no, which is true. Everything's fine. Pretty much. No major problems. And then she says well, she couldn't help but wonder because I seem to be having trouble lately with getting my work done accurately and on time. Which is so not true! I mean, you know how many people we process every day? It's not unusual to occasionally get — not confused, but temporarily lost . . . Overwhelmed. Plus, we're short on staff because of the hiring freeze. We're all working really.

SMOKE AND MIRRORS
Joseph Goodrich

Dramatic
Tammie, twenties to thirties

*Tammie reveals what in her opinion are the real reasons behind the
Iraq War.*

TAMMIE: My Country, 'Tis Of Thee. A country held hostage by a fanatical dictator . . . A country that possesses weapons of mass destruction . . . A country that flouts domestic and international law with impunity . . . A country mad enough to even contemplate the use of nuclear weapons . . A country like this must be held accountable for its actions. The reckless, criminal, amoral behavior of a country like that must be stopped in its tracks. *(Pause.)* My country, 'tis of thee I speak. The merest glance beneath the officially sanctioned news sources reveals without a doubt the real reasons for America's latest rush to war. The real reasons are breathtakingly simple, breathtakingly transparent no matter how cunningly disguised in the bunting of patriotic rhetoric. The United States' quest for Empire, its desire for world-wide hegemony over resources (oil, primarily) and people (who represent the markets that Capitalism demands to further impoverish the poor and make the rich richer). *(Pause.)* In service of this quest, which is supported and rationalized by a worldview as Manichean and apocalyptic as that of the supposed "enemy," there are no depths to which the United States will not sink. Facts will be twisted, the historical record re-written, fustian and bombast will be used to manipulate its wary, frightened citizens. The true destructiveness of war — the way it rips limbs from bodies, heads from torsos, the way men, women and children suffer when wells have no water that isn't contaminated, when depleted uranium wreaks havoc on bones and brains now and into perpetuity, when the gutters run with blood and sewage, when the entire infrastructure of a country's been destroyed — all this will be downplayed, ignored, forgotten. *(Pause.)* In service of this quest fake crises will be created, such as the im — imbro — imbroglio over "weapons of mass destruction," while real, ongoing crises such as the continued persecution of the Palestinian people by the state of Israel with economic and military assistance from the United States, will be downplayed, ignored, forgotten. *(Pause.)* Forgotten, at least, by the ones responsible for the damage and chaos. Those who have no choice but to live in chaos cannot forget. *(Pause.)* This is the challenge we face: How do we change a system that not only thrives on war — the preparations beforehand, the reparations after, the whole ugly process of demolishing and rebuilding that benefits only the demolitionists — but is itself the cause of war? *(Pause.)* How do we change this? *(Pause.)* How? *(Pause.)* How? *(Pause.)* How?

SONGS OF THE DRAGON FLYING HEAVEN

Young Jean Lee

Dramatic
Korean-American Woman, could be any age

Speaker talks about how difficult it is to be Korean in America.

KOREAN-AMERICAN WOMAN: Have you ever noticed how most Asian-Americans are slightly brain-damaged from having grown up with Asian parents?

It's like being raised by monkeys — these retarded monkeys who can barely speak English and are too evil to understand anything besides conformity and status. Most of us hate these monkeys from an early age and try to learn how to be human from school or television, but the result is always tainted by this subtle or not-so-subtle retardation. Asian people from Asia are even more brain-damaged, but in a different way, because they are the original monkey. Anyway, some white men who like Asian women seem to like this retarded quality as well, and sometimes the more retarded the better.

I am so mad about all of the racist things against me in this country, which is America.

Like the fact that the reason why so many white men date Asian women is that they can get better-looking Asian women than they can get white women because we are easier to get and have lower self-esteem. It's like going with an inferior brand so that you can afford more luxury features. Also, Asian women will date white guys who no white woman would touch.

But the important thing about being Korean is getting to know your roots. Because we come to this country and want to forget our ancestry, but this is bad, and we have to remember that our grandfathers and grandmothers were people too, with interesting stories to tell.

Which leads to a story from my grandmother, which is the story of the mudfish.

In Korea they have this weird thing where everyone turns a year older on New Year's day. So if you were born on December 31st, you turn one on January 1st even though you've only been alive for a day. Anyway, each year on New Year's day, my grandmother used to make this special dish called meekudaji tong that she would only serve once a year because it was such a pain in the ass to make.

The main ingredient of meekudaji tong is mudfish, which are these tiny fishes they have in Korea that live on muddy riverbanks and eat mud. Every New Year's day, my grandmother would throw a bunch of mudfish into a bowl of brine, which would make them puke out all their mud until they were shiny clean. Then she would put pieces of tofu on a skillet, heat it up, and throw the live mudfish onto the skillet. The mudfish would frantically burrow inside the pieces of tofu to escape the heat and, voila, stuffed tofu!

White people are so alert to any infringement on their rights. It's really funny. And the reason why it's funny is that minorities have all the power. We can take the word racism and hurl it at people and demolish them and there's nothing you can do to stop us.

I feel so much pity for you right now.

You have no idea what's going on. The wiliness of the Korean is beyond anything that you could ever hope to imagine.

I can promise you one thing, which is that we will crush you. You may laugh now, but remember my words when you and your offspring are writhing under our yoke.

(Pause.)

(Raising her fist.)

Let the Korean dancing begin!

SPAIN
Jim Knabel

Seriocomic
Diversion, thirties

> *Diversion's best friend, Barbara, claims she has a 16th Century Spanish Conquistador in her apartment. Barbara's husband left her for another woman. Then he came home as if nothing had happened, so she stabbed him and killed him. When the police came she stabbed a policeman. Diversion tries to make sense of all of this.*

DIVERSION: Barbara always was a little, you know, out there. But she controlled it. She worked hard at the office. She was very good at talking to people on the phone and dealing with Escrow. But on her lunch breaks, you know, we would talk, I was her best friend — I am her best friend, and she would say things every once in while. "I'm feeling restless." "John doesn't pay attention to me." She had this fantasy about Spain. It started two years ago. She saw a movie or something. She started buying books. Maps. She toyed with taking a Spanish class, but she didn't have time and John was very unsupportive of the whole thing.

I don't blame her for stabbing him. He was a real bastard. She shouldn't be punished too harshly for that. I was more disturbed by the other stabbing. That poor man. He was just doing his job.

TEA
Valina Hasu Houston

Dramatic
Himiko, twenties to thirties

Himiko is telling some other Japanese women about the rape and murder of her daughter.

HIMIKO: It isn't about dating guys. It's about being *fucked* by guys. . . . By everybody: your mother, your father — and even yourself. . . . Don't ask me about my mother. Because then you're asking me about myself . . . and I don't know who the hell I am. . . . I was born in a storm and it's never stopped raining. My only blessing is Mieko, my half-Japanese girl. I love her so much, but she was born in my storm, too. For years, I tried to talk to her, but she wasn't ready. *(A sad laugh.)* Mieko is so fast, I only know what she looks like from behind. Because she's always leaving, her big Japanese o-shiri swaying like a flower, out looking for dreams she thinks men are going to give her. So it was a Saturday in May. Mieko wants to make me worry, so she *hitchhikes*. She's gone three days. Then the big policeman comes. "Do you have a daughter named Mieko? When's the last time you saw her, Mrs. Hamilton?" *(Breathes hard and fast; forces composure.)* The last time I saw Mieko is in the dusk. She looks so Japanese, her shoulders curving like gentle hills. "Perfect kimono shoulders," her grandmother would say. *(A pause.)* Mieko came home today. Someone made her dirty, stabbed her in the chest many times and then raped her as she died. Left a broom inside my little girl's body. Her brassiere was shredded by the knife. *(A pause.)* There is no one for me; there never was. Even my sisters of Japan cannot bless me with sandals to cover my blistered feet as I prepare for the longest journey. *(Looks around.)* Billy, is that you? Before it's too late, tell me the truth. You loved me, didn't you? Once. Once there was nobody like me. Now that I know, I can go on without you, Billy. I see you there, waiting in the mist, your strong arms ready to hold me for one last dance. But I'm going another way. Like bamboo. I sway back and forth in the wind, bending but never breaking. Never again. The war is over. Mother? Is that you? Are you waiting for me, too? *(Brief, absolute delight, addressing Mieko when she was five.)* Mieko-chan, I see you dancing in my best kimono all light and laughter and . . . clean! *(The delight fades.)* No, you all have to let me go now. I have a long walk ahead of me. All ties are unbound, as completely as if they never existed. *(She exits as lights dim.)*

TEMPODYSSEY

Dan Dietz

Dramatic
Genny, twenties to thirties

Genny talks about a terrible job she had in a chicken slaughter-house.

Genny runs into a stall, yanks up her skirt and heaves a huge sigh of relief.

GENNY: I know. I know about morality. I was a chicken-choker.

As in I grabbed chickens firmly by the neck and swung them around in a funky circumference and *cracked their necks.* A human neck is only meant to be turned approximately ninety degrees in either direction. A chicken's is a little more flexible, it can rotate about one hundred and twenty degrees to the right or left. But very few animals have necks that can swivel three hundred and sixty degrees, and even then we're talking it's only supposed to go once. Not twice (seven hundred and twenty degrees). Thrice (one thousand and eighty degrees). Or more, more, more, more, *mooooorrrre! (Crrrrrrrrrrrraack!!! Appalachia. Genny, her drawl creeping in from offstage to gather in the hollows of her mouth, grows younger and younger as we watch.)*

Oh, I was gooooood. I was a little girl, no more'n eight years old, when I choked my first chicken. I'd been watching Daddy getting ready for Thanksgiving, filling orders for all the folks in town who wanted turkey but settled for chicken. He was efficient. He was quick. He was surgical in his precision. The stance: legs slightly more than hip-width apart. Feet planted. Kind of like a baseball batter up at the plate. The grip: fingers firm, real firm, but the rest of the arm loosey-goosey. The chicken is tossed slightly in one direction, for momentum, then begins to fall in the other and is swung in a whipcrack twist and — *(crrrrrrrrrrrrrrrrraaaaccck!!!)*

And a shiver run updown through my spinal column. Like the ghost of that chicken electrocuted me, charged through the holes in my witnessing eyes, shrieked into my brain and surged down my spine and quivered into my legs and *zzzzzzzzzzzaaaap!!!* out my body back into the deep red mountain dirt from whence it came. Dust to dust is oversimplifying the matter. The equation is actually dust to lasergorge lightningsong howlabout hungertrick lipquiver backbanging holyriver huntrunner blacksaddle thundershock hiss-a-bit to dust. But where holy books are concerned, lots of stuff gets lost in translation.

I was a chicken-choker. And this is how it started. Daddy went inside to answer the telephone, take down another chicken order. And I walked on over to the cubical cage he was keeping them in. They were beating their wings, buffeting each other, there was some blood. Daddy didn't usually do this kind of thing, keep them crammed together like that, but for Thanksgiving he had to, the chickens could sense death coming on a mass scale, descending with ripple-fingers to take cold hold of each and every one of them, so the jig was definitely up and the only way to get it done was to just jam them all together in one place and reach and pull and swing and crack and reach and pull and swing and crack and *(Genny is now a little girl.) Reach* and *pull* and *swing* and *crack* and *reach (Genny reaches.)* and *pull (Genny pulls.)* and *swing (Genny swings.)* and *crack!* . . . I broke something.

I broke something.

I broke something!!!

THIS BEAUTIFUL CITY
Steven Cosson and Jim Lewis

Dramatic
Young Woman

*Speaker is talking to an unseen interviewer about how she came to
let God into her life.*

YOUNG WOMAN: — *God's grace*
  We came from a Christian background. My father's father was
a minister, so it was really a shock for all of us when my Dad came
out of the closet. So after my parents divorced, I moved out here to
live with my dad actually. I was just a kid and I wanted my dad you
know? I wanted him to keep loving me. But then my dad's boyfriend
moved in. And I was put on the back burner; he didn't need me. So
I just went wild and did whatever I wanted to. I actually met my
husband when I'd just turned sixteen and within a few months I was
living with him. My dad was like, whatever! A week after I turned
seventeen, my dad signed for us to get married, and then left for
California. Yeah he left right after. Really fast right after.
  . . . Guys. Guys. Keep it down please Mom is talking to someone. Anyhow, my husband and I lived in Manitou Springs then. *(A
little quieter.)* There was constant drug use, for lack of a better way
to put it. I can probably count the days of sobriety on two hands.
My husband and I had a really short bout with crystal meth, I'd say
three months. And it must have been the grace of God, 'cause I've
heard that it's really hard to get off of. And the day before, a Saturday
night, my husband and I were actually at a strip club, a local strip
club, and we were doing coke with a bunch of strippers — I dunno,
it was a party night. We had a baby sitter. And I guess I had just been
very gently hearing God calling to me, because and the next morning I got up, and I got the kids dressed, and I walked them to this
church down the road, Revolution Church. Just like that, and it was

funny. I mean, look where I'd been just a few hours before. And it was unlike anything I had ever been to before. They had like strobe lights and a smoke machine and a disco ball! And the people there were so friendly and they were my age and they had tattoos! And I was sitting there with my boys, just crying, and it was kind of embarrassing cause I was crying in front of my boys. And I just felt that I just didn't realize that I had missed God! And I said, God, who am I to you? And he just revealed to me, "You are my daughter, my beloved, you're my beautiful flower, you're the one that pleases me." And in a way it made me ashamed of all the years that I had lived, not, for the way that he had intended for me? But at the same time he just lifted that burden off of me. He freed me, and just revealed to me that it was ok. And it made his heart ache every time I made a poor choice, but he loved me nonetheless, and he wasn't willing to let me go. *(Big tears.)* I'm sorry, something's got to give when you are face to face with God, when he's consuming you. Some people fall to their knees, some people cry out. I just start to leak.

But it's funny, if I had just walked into some boring church, I would still be sitting on the couch smoking pot. We really liked Revolution and are still really good friends with the leaders, but it went from being a church to being a 24-hour house of prayer. Just prayer all the time. By the time we left it had gone from like 150 members to twelve or something. We just needed more of a community. That's when we chose New Life. Yeah, Revolution House of Prayer. RHOP, right. Oh you've been there? What did you think?

UNCONDITIONAL

Brett C. Leonard

Dramatic
Jessica, thirties

*Jessica tells a friend about an incident in her childhood in which a
neighborhood bully got his just desserts.*

JESSICA: Every bully in the world's a big fat pussy underneath. At ele-
mentary school when I was growin' up there was this Italian bully
kid named Ronnie Mancini who useta beat the shit outta every
kid on the playground. The cafeteria, the classrooms, it didn't matter ta this little prick. So one day, there's this kid named Bruce
Tompkinson — nerdy, red-hair, freckles, got braces on his teeth an'
he's walkin' with those whaddaya call — those two metal walker
crutch-type things with the metal arm braces. Totally atrophied
legs, all fucked-up, skinny like two chop-stix, but loose — not
chop stix, like a coupla lo-mein noodles, and his feet all contorted
an' twisted-up-crooked an' shit, draggin' all behind him an' shit, and
he's wearin' this Cub Scout uniform with lil' tassles an' ribbons on
it — lil' yellow tassles an' pleated shorts, yo, this the Bronx 1982 —
so this Ronnie Mancini, this Guinea bully kid, he comes up to'm
one day — this gotta be, what, fourth-fifth grade maybe — he's
already terrorized the whole fuckin' neighborhood since kinder-
garten — both his uncles an' ol' man are Made Men on Arthur
Avenue, blah-blah-blah — how's your coffee? — my shit's always
cold in this place — they put a Starbucks in Harlem it's like "fuck
'em, them niggas don't know from coffee." So this Ronnie the
Dago, he walks over ta lil' crippled Brucie Tompkinson an' he steals
one a' his metal walker thingies, Brucie goes down, starts crawlin'
towards this chain-link fence — Ronnie Mancini meanwhile he's
limpin' around all retarded-like, makin' fun a' poor lil' Brucie.
Nobody *else's* laughin', but Ronnie Mancini can't fuckin' *stop*

laughin' — limpin' around, feet draggin' all over the place — makin' fun a' the physically impaired — totally fucked up — then Brucie, both arms grabbin' hold a' the fence, his little crutch dan-glin' — he comes sneakin', *creepin'*, like a horror movie Zombie with flaming red hair, and outta nowhere — outta fuckin' *nowhere* — with some shit he musta learned in the Cub Scouts, he takes the *other* crutch-thing an' cracks the shit outta Ronnie right to his bully-wop-dago-fuck-head — whack — right ta the temple — blood splurtin' all over the place — *now* the other kids start laughin' — but here's the thing . . . Ronnie Mancini? This bully bitch never shows his face around school ever again — never — that's that. One lil' crack ta the side a' the brain from a redheaded cripple retarded kid an' the biggest bully in the Bronx was a bully no more. One blow, Trace — one shot.

WELCOME HOME, JENNY SUTTER

Julie Marie Myatt

Dramatic
Jenny, thirties

> *Jenny is on the run from an abusive husband. She is looking for*
> *something to believe in.*

JENNY: I was born in a one-room apartment over the family Exxon
Station in Barstow, California. As a baby, I liked to sit in my father's
arms and look out the window. Always facing forward. Both our
eyes looking out on the day. "Show me the way, Dad. Guide me.
Show me how to live in that world." With my mother, I preferred
to sit as close as possible to her chest, heart to heart, not caring what
I saw. Not needing to see a thing but her. "Teach me how to love,
Mom. Let me feel what love feels like." And when I couldn't sit in
either of their arms, because they were too busy floundering apart,
I would lay facing the ceiling in my crib. My eyes darting back and
forth against the white paint, looking for cracks. "Are you there,
God? Is that God up there? Hey, God, if you are up there, can you
give me something to believe in? Just come through the cracks and
talk to me, OK?" But. The ceiling was quiet. The ceiling never
changed. Only the same shadows of my parents dancing across the
white, as they stood arguing in a corner of the room . . . Eventually,
I stopped asking. I gave up on the ceiling. I turned my face to the
wall instead, where there hung a picture of my dead uncle Jim,
killed in Vietnam. Slowly I fell asleep in the comfort of his young,
beautiful smile . . . the flickering light of the gold buttons on his
proud chest . . . and I dreamed of being a hero.

WHAT SHALL I DO FOR PRETTY GIRLS?

Don Nigro

Seriocomic
Iseult Gonne, twenty-three

> *Iseult is the illegitimate daughter of a French politician and Maud*
> *Gonne, the Irish actress and political activist. She is walking on the*
> *Normandy coast of France with her mother's friend, the great Irish*
> *poet William Butler Yeats, age fifty-one, who's been in love with*
> *Maud for many years, and has always been like a father to Iseult,*
> *whose stepfather MacBride has molested her. Now Yeats, anxious to*
> *settle down and have children, and rejected by Maud once again,*
> *has come to ask Iseult to marry him. It's 1917, the First World War*
> *is raging not far away. Iseult is very smart, artistically gifted, beau-*
> *tiful and charming, with a dark sense of humor, and she loves Yeats,*
> *but she has some very mixed feelings about his shift from father fig-*
> *ure to possible husband, and is not sure who she is or what she*
> *wants to be. Maud insists that Iseult call her Moura rather than*
> *Mother so people will think they're sisters.*

ISEULT: You've just admitted you'd like to kiss me. So why don't you? Of course, Romantic love is not a good idea. Sex is a terrible idea. And yet none of us would be here without that illusion and that obscenity. You treat me as if I were some sort of innocent, but I'm not. I've seen horrible things, nursing the wounded. Monstrous things. And not just penises, either. I've observed first hand the steaming offal that lurks and throbs inside us. What a mess. It's made me quite grown up. And I'm not stupid, you know. I was making excellent progress in my study of Bengali until my Indian tutor tried to persuade me to take off my clothes to demonstrate the Kama Sutra positions. Moura had to be restrained from neutering him with the garden shears. Not to speak, of course, of my violent molestation by my step-father. We never speak of that. I still have nightmares about him. I'm afraid to climb the staircase. I imagine he'll jump out from behind the clock and grab me. He used to lurk in the house, lying in wait for me. He pretended it was a game. Let's play, he said. Beautiful Iseult, he said. Let's play. I still dream that he's running after me through an old dark house full of clocks. He's the king of the great clock tower. And yet Moura didn't actually get around to throwing him out until he'd raped her sister. She knew. It just wasn't convenient for her to acknowledge that she knew. There's no end to the monstrosities that men will commit. He used to beat Mother up. You wouldn't think a big strong woman like Moura would let a nasty little man like that beat her up, but the ugly truth is, she was drawn to his violence. He slept with anything that moved, and some that didn't. But he was a great man in the Irish resistance, so of course he could do no wrong. All men are insane, and most of the women. That's my philosophy. I've had a terrible crush on you since I was a girl, you know. But in my heart I'm old, and getting older every minute. In a matter of weeks I shall most likely be a ninety-year old Hindu gentleman. But if you asked me to marry you, I might say yes.

WHEN THE MESSENGER IS HOT

Marisa Wegrzyn

Dramatic
Josie 1, twenties

*In this play Josie is played by three different actresses. Her mother
has recently died and here she is telling us of her realization of the
finality of her death.*

JOSIE: *(Fast and furious.)* I know what you're thinking. You're thinking
this is the part where I realize, via a simple metaphor, that my
mother is not coming back, the part where I snap out of denial and
realize that there will be no big reunion, that she will not send me
vitamins or make me chicken soup again when I'm sick, or buy me
a new teakettle when mine gets rusty . . .

   Where I realize that we will never go outlet shopping again,
never decorate another Christmas tree, that we will never again giggle uncontrollably about my cousin's famously cheap Christmas
presents. The part where I understand that she will never come to
Chicago again and we will not have coffee on my porch, that she'll
never get to meet Connor or Lisa or Tracy or my great new
boyfriend (hypothetical) and that they'll never get to meet her. The
part where I realize that I will never get to ask her all the questions
I want to ask her, like how do you knit a popcorn stitch, like what's
the exact basil-to-oregano ratio for the perfect marinara, like how
come I have no brothers or sisters, like what was I like as a kid and
what were you like and what was Grandma like then . . . and what
was it that made you so sad sometimes. The part where I realize that
I will never get to tell her that even though she was completely crazy
that I would never in a million years want another Mom, that even
Mrs. C. would pale in comparison. The part where I finally understand why my mother wasn't there to help me get through my

mother's death, because it still makes perfect sense to me that any-one would need their mom at a time like that.

(A beat.)

But it *isn't*.

(A beat.)

It's the part where I go to North Dakota and drive to every bus station south of Minot with a picture of my Mom.

(Josie approaches unseen North Dakota people.)

Excuse me, have you seen this woman? Excuse me, this is a picture of my mother who is missing, you haven't seen her, have you?

WHITE PEOPLE
JT Rogers

Dramatic
Mara Lynn, twenties

Mara Lynn tells us the sad story of her marriage.

MARA LYNN: Oh, you should have seen me when I went off to Fayetteville
State! I was the toast, I was the belle of the ball. I mean, the clothes
I'd wear, the things I could get away with! Crossing the campus,
strutting in high-heel patent leather and angora sweaters, all snowy
white and pillow soft. Hair down, miniskirt up, pink lipstick: I
looked wicked good. I dropped out midway through sophomore
year. All those lectures, tests — I had boys' eyes burning into my
hips down any street I walked. What more does a life need?

Besides, I had my Elm. I had a man who was gonna take care
of me. He was so handsome when we were married. White tuxedo,
silver bow tie. Shaved his face for me, clean and smooth. Life was
gonna be one long stretch in the summer sun. All Earl had to do
was get focused, get on with his life.

See the year before, Elm Doddson was gonna take his fifty-two
and three record to the state championships and on to Iowa State.
That's God's country for wrestlers. That's till he tore out his knee in
the district final. Ripped it away from the bone. Fifty-two and three
will take you to Iowa, but fifty-two and three and a limp and you're
just like everybody else.

After the wedding I pushed and prodded, got him to enroll at
Fayetteville Tech. Mechanical Engineering. He was gonna be a
damn good one, too. What he used to do, souping up his daddy's
. . . *(Pause.)* See, he didn't have anyone helping him. His teachers
didn't know who he was. They hadn't walked through the halls of
Southview. They hadn't seen how people stepped aside when he
passed, watched how when he moved it was like he was partin'

water. Earl tried, he just . . . He just didn't know how. I don't hold that against him. Other things. But not that.

Listen to this now. This is what you call advice. When you fix on a man, you make sure and lock onto something steady. Something's gonna be there in the long haul. Year after year, beer after beer, those beautiful ridges that trapped my heart . . . Well, they just melted away. Elm was gone. I was left with Earl. *(Looks around her.)* I was left with all this.

RIGHTS AND PERMISSIONS

Please note:
Performance rights holder is also the source for the complete text.

AND HER HAIR WENT WITH HER. © 2007 by Zina Camblin. Reprinted by permission of Mary Harden, Harden-Curtis Assoc. For performance rights, contact Dramatists Play Service, 440 Park Ave. S., New York, NY 10016 (www.dramatists.com).

. . . AND WE ALL WORE LEATHER PANTS. © 2008 by Robert Attenweiler. Reprinted by permission of the author (rattenweiler@hotmail.com). The entire text has been published by New York Theatre Experience (www.nytheatre.com) in *Plays and Playwrights* 2008.

BEAUTY OF THE FATHER. © 2007 by Nilo Cruz. Reprinted by permission of Peregrine Whittlesey Agency. For performance rights, contact Dramatists Play Service, 440 Park Ave. S., New York, NY 10016 (www.dramatists.com).

THE BEEBO BRINKER CHRONICLES. © 2008 by Kate Moira Ryan and Linda S. Chapman. Reprinted by permission of Beth Blickers, Abrams Artists Agency. For performance rights, contact Beth Blickers (beth.blickers@abramsart.com).

BOATS ON A RIVER. © 2008 by Julie Marie Myatt. Reprinted by permission of Bruce Ostler, Bret Adams Ltd. For performance rights, contact Bruce Ostler (bostler@bretadams.com).

A BODY OF WATER. © 2007 by Lee Blessing. Reprinted by permission of Judy Boals, Inc. For performance rights, contact Dramatists Play Service, 440 Park Ave. S., New York, NY 10016 (www.dramatists.com).

BOOM. © 2008 by Peter Sinn Nachtrieb. Reprinted by permission of Bruce Ostler, Bret Adams Ltd. For performance rights, contact Bruce Ostler (bostler@bretadams.com).

THE BUTCHER OF BARABOO. © 2007 by Marisa Wegrzyn. Reprinted by permission of Morgan Jenness, Abrams Artists Agency. For performance rights, contact Morgan Jenness (morgan.jenness@abramsart.com). The entire text has been published by Smith and Kraus, Inc. in *New Playwrights: The Best Plays of 2008.*

CHRISTMAS BELLES. © 2008 by Jessie Jones, Nicholas Hope and Jamie Wooten. Reprinted by permission of the authors. For performance rights, contact Dramatists Play Service, 440 Park Ave. S., New York, NY 10016 (www.dramatists.com).

CHRONICLES SIMPKINS WILL CUT YOUR ASS OFF. © 2008 by Rolin Jones. Reprinted by permission of Chris Till, Paradigm Agency. For performance rights, contact Chris Till (ctill@paradigmagency.com).

THE CONSCIENTIOUS OBJECTOR. Michael Murphy. Reprinted by permission of Chris Till, Paradigm Agency. For performance rights, contact Chris Till (ctill@paradigmagency.com).

CUSTODY OF THE EYES (2). © 2008 by Anthony Giardina. Reprinted by permission of Bruce Ostler, Bret Adams Ltd. For performance rights, Dramatists Play Service, 440 Park Ave. S., New York, NY 10016 (www.dramatists.com).

THE DRUNKEN CITY. © 2008 by Adam Bock. Reprinted by permission of Val Day, William Morris Agency LLC. For performance rights, contact Samuel French, Inc. 45 W. 25th St., New York, NY 10010 (www.samuelfrench.com).

EARTHQUAKE CHICA. © 2008 by Anne García-Romero. Reprinted by permission of The Susan Gurman Agency. For performance rights, contact Broadway Play Publishing, 56 E. 81st St., New York, NY 10021 (www.broadwayplaypubl.com).

EAT THE RUNT. © 2008 by Avery Crozier. Reprinted by permission of the Joan Scott Agency. For performance rights, contact Broadway Play Publishing, 56 E. 81st St., New York, NY 10021 (www.broadwayplaypubl.com).

ELLIOT, A SOLDIER'S FUGUE. © 2007 by Quiara Alegría Hudes. Reprinted by permission of Bruce Ostler, Bret Adams Ltd. For performance rights, contact Dramatists Play Service, 440 Park Ave. S., New York, NY 10016 (www.dramatists.com).

FALL FORWARD. © 2008 by Daniel Reitz. Reprinted by permission of the author. For performance rights, contact the author (dereitz@earthlink.net).

FOOD FOR FISH. © 2007 by Adam Szymkowicz. Reprinted by permission of Pat McLaughlin, Beacon Artists Agency. For performance rights, contact Broadway Play Publishing, 56 E. 81st St., New York, NY 10021 (www.broadwayplaypubl.com).